MEDIT [T5-CCV-130]

by

Burns K. Seeley, Ph.D.

Nihil Obstat: Rev. John A. Hardon, S.J.
Censor Deputatus
Imprimatur: Rev. Msgr. John F. Donoghue
Vicar General of the Archdiocese of Washington, D.C.
October 15, 1981

Library of Congress Card Number 82-072201

ISBN Number 0-932406-06-8

Item number for this book is 323-77
The Apostolate, Box 220, Kenosha, WI 53141

File in
The Apostolate's Prayerbook
Book A4-1, Behind Section 2, Chapter 110

or

Living Meditation and Prayerbook Series
Book A4-3, Behind Section C2, Chapter 102

Structured by Jerome F. Coniker
Edited by Dale Francis

Published by
The Apostolate for Family Consecration
The Apostolate, Box 220
Kenosha, Wisconsin 53141

International Center
Arlington, Virginia

Printed in U.S.A.

This book and the entire
Meditations on St. Paul
Peace of Heart Forums
are dedicated to
St. Joseph
for the renewal of family life
throughout the world.

Table of Contents

Act of Consecration

Heavenly Father, grant that we, who are nourished by the Body and Blood of Your Divine Son, may die to our own selfishness and be one spirit with Christ, as we seek to fulfill Your distinctive plan for our lives.

Form me and all the members of my family, community, and the Apostolate, into instruments of atonement. Unite our entire lives with the Holy Sacrifice of Jesus in the Mass of Calvary, and accept our seed sacrifice offering of all of our spiritual and material possessions, for the Sacred and Eucharistic Heart of Jesus, through the Sorrowful and Immaculate Heart of Mary, in union with St. Joseph.

Our Father, let Sacred Scripture's Four "C's" of Confidence, Conscience, seed-Charity, and Constancy, be our guide for living our consecration as peaceful children and purified instruments of the Most Holy Family.

Let us live our consecration by remaining perpetually confident, calm, cheerful, and compassionate, especially with the members of our own family and community.

Please protect our loved ones and ourselves from the temptations of the world, the flesh, and the devil. Help us to become more sensitive to the inspirations of Your Holy Spirit, the Holy Family, our Patron Saints, and Guardian Angels.

And now, Most Heavenly Father, inspire us

1

to establish the right priorities for Your precious gift of time. And most of all, help us to be more sensitive to the needs and feelings of our loved ones.

Never let us forget the souls in Purgatory who are dependent upon us for help. Enable us to gain for the Poor Souls of our loved ones and others, as many indulgences as possible. We ask You this, Our Father, in the name of Our Lord and Savior Jesus Christ, Your Son and the Son of Mary. Amen.

Cenacle Prayer

'To Be Recited Before All AFC Gatherings

Our Father, we gather together in the Name of Your Son Jesus Christ, and ask You to cast out all the demons coming against our families and the Apostolate for Family Consecration.

We entrust this gathering to the Sorrowful and Immaculate Heart of Mary, in union with St. Joseph. And through the intercession of our Patrons, especially that of St. Vincent Pallotti, the Patron of all lay apostolates, we ask You to enable us, personally and collectively, to fulfill Your distinctive plan for our lives.

Father, we offer You the Precious Body, Blood, Soul and Divinity of Your Son, Our Lord Jesus Christ, in atonement for all of our sins and the sins of our families, neighborhoods, country and the entire world.

Most Holy Spirit, inspire, and protect us from pride, error and division. Bless our Holy Father the Pope, our Bishops and Priests. Also bless the activities and members of the Apostolate in this area.

Most Sacred and Eucharistic Heart of Jesus, pour Your Precious Blood down upon our families and the universal work of the Apostolate for Family Consecration. We particularly pray for the petitions placed at the foot of the Altar in our Sacred Hearts Chapel at the House of St. Joseph.

We ask all of this in Your Name, through the Immaculate Heart of our Mother Mary, in union with the Head of the Holy Family, St. Joseph. Amen.

Seed-Charity Prayer in the Spirit
of St. Francis

Lord, make me an instrument of your peace;
Where there is hatred, let me sow seeds of
love;
Where there is injury, let me sow seeds of
pardon;
Where there is discord, let me sow seeds of
union;
Where there is doubt, let me sow seeds of
faith;
Where there is despair, let me sow seeds of
hope;
Where there is darkness, let me sow seeds of
light;
And where there is sadness, let me sow seeds
of joy.
O Divine Master, grant that I may not so
much seek to be consoled as to console You
in others;
To be loved, as to love You in others;
For it is in *giving that we receive.*
It is in pardoning that we are pardoned,
And it is in *dying as a seed to our selfishness
that we are born to eternal life.*

Prayer to St. Joseph for The Apostolate

St. Joseph, place me in the presence of the Blessed Sacrament of the altar in the Sacred Hearts Chapel, at the House of St. Joseph, and unite my prayers with those of the other members and friends of the society of the Apostolate for Family Consecration throughout the world.

We know, St. Joseph, that Our Lord will refuse you nothing. Please ask God to bless the Apostolate and all of its members and friends. Ask Our Lord to help the Apostolate accomplish its goal of establishing an international network of permanent chapters of dedicated volunteers. Ask Jesus to use these chapters to transform neighborhoods into God-centered communities by thoroughly educating people in the spiritual life.

St. Joseph, we are confident that you will remove all obstacles in the path of this spiritual renewal program, so that our society will be transformed through a chain reaction that will renew the family, the neighborhood, the school and the Church.

Form the society of the Apostolate for Family Consecration into a useful instrument of the Holy Family, and never let its members and leaders falsely judge others or fall into the sin of pride or complacency in success, which is so fatal to the work of God. Use the Apostolate as an instrument to bring about the social reign of the Sacred Heart of Jesus and the Immaculate Heart of Mary in our age. Amen.

Come Holy Spirit

Come, Holy Spirit, Who resides in the innermost recesses of my soul and give me the light of Your wisdom through the fire of Your divine love.

INTRODUCTION

1. Before you begin to meditate on the five letters of St. Paul contained in this book, we would like you to read these introductory pages since they will help you make fruitful meditations.

2. We will share with you some suggestions on how to meditate well, and we will give you some background information on St. Paul and on his letters. This should help you to better understand the man and the message of salvation he conveys.

3.   Within the pages of Paul's letters we are especially eager for you to meditate on what the Apostolate calls Scripture's Four C's. Why? Because, if they are applied to your life, you will enjoy that inner peace which only God can give.

Scripture's Four C's

4.   What are Scripture's Four C's? Those of you who are already acquainted with the work of the Apostolate for Family Consecration will no doubt already know the answer, especially if you have read Volume I of Jerome Coniker's two volume work called "Scripture's Four C's Formula for Peaceful Seed Living" and his "Prayers and Recommended Practices" book. *(For information on the work and goals of the Apostolate see pp. 247)*

5.   Confidence, Conscience, seed-Charity and Constancy. These are the four pillars of the *Peaceful Seed-Living Formula.* And, we hope they will become a permanent part of your life so you will always have ready access to that God-given peace which defies complete understanding.

Confidence (C-1)

6.   The first C - "Confidence." When we speak of "Confidence," what do we mean? We mean a supernaturally-given trust in God, a trust in His unique plan for each of us, and a trust in the strength He will give us to accomplish this plan. Since God is completely good, He desires only what is best for us, namely, our interior peace. But if we are to obtain this inner peace of heart, our trust or confidence, must be focused on Him.

8

7.   We also mean by confidence, a super-naturally-given ability to believe the truths which the Father has revealed for our salvation through the patriarchs, the prophets, the Apostles, and especially through Jesus. When we use confidence to mean this type of belief, we are using it in the same way that "faith" is used in most of the New Testament, that is, in the exclusively Christian part of the Bible.

8.   Less frequently, we use confidence to mean hope, that is, hope in eternal life with God, hope in the rewards that accompany eternal life and hope in the means of obtaining it.

9.   It can be seen then, that we use confidence as a synonym for trust, faith and hope, which are special graces mentioned often in the New Testament and given by God for our salvation.

10.   To sum up, The Apostolate speaks of confidence as trust in God, belief in His supernaturally revealed truths, hope in eternal life, and hope in the means to obtain it.

Conscience (C-2)

11.   Now, the second C - "Conscience." As used by the Apostolate for Family Consecration, conscience means a pure conscience, or one that is free from all fully deliberate sins, since these are the major obstacles to spiritual growth and a life of union or oneness with God.

12.   Imperfections and half deliberate sins,

on the other hand, while they do not prevent us from enjoying God's friendship and a pure conscience, are nonetheless obstacles to obtaining a purer conscience, and can therefore be sources of spiritual illnesses leading to mortal sins. Consequently, we should, with the aid of God's grace, seek to remove them, too, along with all willfull sins.

13. Through Scripture, we are counselled to purify our consciences by repenting of our sins so we can grow in holiness and in God's friendship. In order to accomplish this properly, a daily in-depth self-examination for these hindrances to holiness should be undertaken.

Seed-Charity (C-3)

14. Next, our third C - "seed-Charity." Seed-charity or seed-sacrifice, or we could say seed-love, is that grace referred to in the Bible which makes it possible for us to offer ourselves fully to the true service of God and our fellow man. Put another way, we could say seed-charity enables us to love God as He

commanded us to do with all our hearts, with all our souls, with all our minds, and with all our strength, and to love our neighbor as ourselves. Indeed, seed-charity enables us to love others as Christ has loved us, that is, even to the point of death.

15. We of the Apostolate prefer the term "seed-charity" to simply "charity" or "love," since in modern English it is not always clear what these latter two terms mean. Thus when we prefix "seed" to charity, we wish to convey the idea of a love which is essentially sacrificial. Without this prefix, charity is often thought of solely in terms of donating time or money to some worthy cause. But activity of this sort is not always sacrificial. Also, the word "love" without the prefix "seed" could mean either romantic love or the love of casual friendship, but neither of these needs to be sacrificial either.

16.   If we were to reflect on it, we would all realize a seed is meant to sacrifice itself, or die, so a new life, that of a plant, might slowly emerge and eventually achieve full growth. Similarly, one who exercises sacrificial love or seed-charity dies to his selfishness, so a new Christ-like individual can emerge and ultimately attain full growth in sanctity through a transforming union with Our Lord.

17.   We do not have to look further than our own immediate environment to know where we should plant our seeds of sacrificial charity. And in doing so, we are faithfully fulfilling our responsibilities in our state in life. Trials, for instance, which come upon all of us, can be sanctified by offering them to God in the spirit of seed-charity. When we plant seeds of sacrifice to meet our spiritual needs in this life, we are preparing ourselves for eternal life with God in His heavenly Kingdom. We are also achieving *peaceful seed-living* on earth, and we are having our material and emotional needs met as well.

Constancy (C-4)

18.   Finally, the fourth C - "Constancy." By constancy we mean a special supernatural grace which allows us to persevere with a pure conscience in the Christian life, even during moments of difficult temptations. We need this grace to persevere in all acts which lead to our destiny in Heaven, but especially in the exercise of confidence and seed-charity.

19.   Constancy is living in God's presence. It is a constant vigilance always to do the things that please God. This includes maintaining a positive attitude of expectation for God's love, for responses to our prayers, and for God's harvest from the charitable seeds we have planted. In a certain sense we cay say constancy is the most important of all virtues, since it undergirds and reinforces all the others. Without it, all of our efforts would bear little spiritual fruit.

The Four C's

20.   Now let's condense and simplify our definitions of the Four C's. Confidence refers to those graces which make it possible for us to trust and hope in God, and also to believe all the truths He has revealed supernaturally for our salvation.

21.   By conscience, we normally mean a conscience which is pure or free of all fully deliberate sins and aware of one's faults to be overcome.

22.   Seed-charity is the supernatural ability to sacrifice ourselves for God by loving Him directly through prayer and worship, and also in our neighbor. We love God too by fulfilling our responsibilities and changing our trials into positive seeds of sacrifice.

23.   Finally, there is constancy which is a special God-given aid that helps us persevere in the fulfillment of our Christian responsibilities and be alert to God's harvest sent our way to fulfill our needs so we can do His will on earth and finally obtain Heaven.

Meditation

24.   Making good meditations is crucial for proper spiritual development. That is why they are an integral part of the Apostolate's spiritual leadership programs.

25.   In general, we could say that a spiritual meditation consists simply in making a prayerful reflection on some spiritual topic or topics with the purpose of knowing and loving God better.

26.   Sacred Scripture or, for that matter, any number of excellent spiritual books, can serve as focal points for meditating since they are rich sources of spiritual subject matter. We would recommend first and foremost, however, the use of Sacred Scripture, inasmuch as it is the primary source book of Christian spirituality.

27.   Over the centuries, the Church has highly recommended scriptural meditation. The Second Vatican Council (1962-1965),

for example, spoke of scriptural meditation as a means of dialoguing with God. Thus it noted that we speak to God when we pray and we listen to Him when we read (and meditate on) His written Word. *("Dogmatic Constitution on Divine Revelation," #25.)*

28. What are the main steps in a scriptural meditation? First, a quiet place should be found — ideally in a church in the presence of the Blessed Sacrament. But, for many, this may not be practical on a regular basis. Consequently, you might choose an isolated area in your home, such as a bedroom.

29. It would be helpful to start your meditation with a prayer to Mary, the Spouse of the Holy Spirit, for help in making your meditation fruitful. And if you have not already done so, it would be well to examine your conscience and confess your sins so there will be no obstacles to the action of God's grace within you. One more thing — it is best to meditate at the same time each day. This makes it easier for meditation to become a habit and, therefore, a normal part of your life.

30. Now, placing the Scripture reading you are going to meditate on in front of you, you should be ready to begin. It is best to read slowly and deliberately, and if you feel moved to do so, to pause from time to time, to reflect on the sentences or passage just read.

31. What do they mean? What is God saying to you and to your families through

them? What acts of charity do they suggest? Perhaps they suggest more fervent prayers, or greater generosity to those closest to you, or some special act of seed-charity for someone you have wrongfully injured.

32. Also when meditating try to find within the Scripture readings, words and ideas which suggest the Four C's. You will probably be surprised to see how often they occur. Confidence, as we have already mentioned, can be seen in words such as "faith," "hope" and "trust." Conscience, or a pure conscience, is suggested immediately by terms such as a "pure heart," and an "honest and good heart." And it is suggested indirectly by many references to sins which must be repented of before a pure conscience can be secured. The idea of seed-charity is found especially in the frequent use of "love" — and the concept of constancy can be found in the use of words such as "persevere" and "endure."

33. Note also in the margin of your Scripture readings, the numbered C's. C-1 represents confidence. C-2 stands for conscience. C-3 stands for seed-charity, C-4 represents constancy, and C-5 represents a combination of the Four C's. These are guides for you in discovering the Four C's in the adjacent Scripture passages. You will undoubtedly discover other references to them as well.

34. It is important that your meditations be forms of prayer, and the subject matter of each prayer should be whatever the Holy Spirit suggests to you while meditating. Perhaps you will be led to express sorrow for your sins, or gratitude for having a loving God Who was willing to become man to suffer and die for each of us. Or reflecting on Scripture may bring to mind those who could use your prayers and other sacrificial acts.

35. During the three weeks of the present spiritual formation program, when you have completed your daily meditation on Scripture, read the prepared companion meditation in the same slow, deliberate manner. This is found immediately following the Scripture reading.

36. The purpose of using the companion meditations is to give you additional insights into the meaning of God's written word for yourself, your family and others.

37. We suggest that if you have not meditated regularly before that, at first, you spend

only fifteen to twenty minutes a day in meditation. Then we recommend you work your way up to a half hour and then perhaps to an hour, both of which will quite likely seem to pass rather quickly. Set your own pace and ask Mary, the Spouse of the Holy Spirit, to take you by the hand and lead you into the spiritual life.

St. Paul

38. Now let's learn something about St. Paul. A contemporary of the other Apostles, although not a member of the original band of twelve, St. Paul was born outside of Palestine in the Jewish section of Tarsus, the capital city of the Roman province of Cilicia, now a part of modern Turkey. His Jewish name was Saul, after the first king of Israel. Paul, a Roman name, was given him, some believe, because of his Roman citizenship inherited from his father.

39.   St. Paul's early formal education seems to have been exclusively Jewish, and more particularly Pharisaic; the Pharisees being a Jewish sect favoring the strict observance of the Jewish or Mosiac Law. Although reared as an observant Jew, we should not conclude that St. Paul was ignorant of the pagan learning and culture which flourished in his native Tarsus, since echoes of it are found in his writings. This knowledge would later prove helpful in his efforts at converting pagans to Christianity.

40.   In his youth, Paul spoke two languages, Aramaic and Greek. The former, spoken also by Jesus, was the first language of the more tradition-oriented Jews of the Near East. The latter was the language used in the synagogues of the Mediterranean world, and by Paul in his New Testament writings. Later, when he received more advanced education in Jerusalem, he learned Hebrew as well.

41.   In Jerusalem, he studied under Gamaliel, a highly respected rabbi and

Pharisee. Under Gamaliel's direction, St. Paul mastered Jewish lore, including distinctively Jewish methods of argumentation, which he would subsequently use as a Christian in attempts at converting his fellow Jews.

42. As a Pharisee and rabbi, Paul labored strenuously for the integrity of traditional Jewish doctrine and for the strict observance of the Mosaic Law.

43. Moreover, he often supported himself, both as a Pharisee and later as a Christian, not by performing his religious duties, but as a textile worker engaged in the manufacture of tents and cloaks.

44. When Jesus ascended into Heaven, and the Apostles, recently filled with the power of the Holy Spirit, were beginning to spread the Gospel throughout the world, Paul, or Saul, was still a practicing Jew. As a matter of fact, he regarded the first Christians as followers of a false messiah and a genuine threat to the Mosaic Law. Thus, he zealously sought to persecute them, as we learn from the Acts of the Apostles.

45. "Meanwhile Saul was still breathing threats to slaughter the Lord's disciples. He had gone to the high priest and asked for letters addressed to the synagogues in Damascus, that would authorize him to arrest and take to Jerusalem any followers of the Way (i.e., followers of Christ), men or women, that he could find." (Acts 9:1-2) It was on his way to Damascus, on fire with

hatred for Christianity, that his unparalleled conversion experience occurred. On the outskirts of the city, he encountered a vision of the Risen Lord, Who said, "Saul, Saul, why are you persecuting me?... I am Jesus and you are persecuting me. Get up now and go to the city and you will be told what you have to do." (Acts 9:4-6) Saul then fell to the ground and was blinded for three days.

46. Arriving in Damascus, he was met by a Jewish Christian named Ananias who had been told by Our Lord in a vision to find Paul. "'This man', said Jesus, 'is my chosen instrument to bring my name before pagans and pagan kings and before the people of Israel; I myself will show him how much he will suffer for my name.'" (Acts 9:15-16)

47. As an Apostle, St. Paul spent the rest of his life tirelessly spreading the Gospel, establishing the Church, and administering the sacraments to both Jewish and Gentile Christians. Continually suffering in the service of Our Lord and His Church, St. Paul's life ended in martyrdom in Rome about A.D. 67.

48.　Now we want to share with you some of the characteristics of St. Paul's fourteen New Testament letters or epistles.

49.　In general, Paul wrote in the pagan style of the period. Thus, all but one of the letters contains an introductory paragraph which includes the name of the writer, the name of the individual or individuals to whom it was written and also a word of greeting. The main body of his letters contains the principal message, followed by a concluding paragraph giving messages from friends and the author's farewell.

50.　In place of the standard pagan greeting of "health," however, St. Paul normally used the salutation, "grace and peace," and in two of his letters, "mercy." In the concluding sections of his writings, he exchanges the pagan "farewell" for variations of "the grace of our Lord Jesus Christ be with you."

51.　In most of St. Paul's letters, the main body has two sections, the first dealing with doctrinal matters and his relationship with those to whom he is writing. The second section pertains to practical problems which he was asked to resolve.

52.　Normally, St. Paul dictated his epistles and would sometimes add a sentence or two at the end in his own handwriting. But, as in the case of his Letter to Philemon, he would on occasion write an entire letter himself.

53. As noted above all of St. Paul's New Testament letters were written in Greek, but not the Greek used by the more learned of the day. Rather it more closely resembled that used in ordinary conversation.

54. The doctrine found in St. Paul's letters was derived in part from divine revelation given to him directly, but in most instances it came from the following sources:

A. From contact with the Apostles and disciples of Our Lord, who were with Him while He was on earth.

B. Reflection on the Old Testament in the light of Christian revelation.

C. His vast knowledge of Jewish teaching.

55. As noted above, in this particular spiritual development program we are asking you to meditate on five of St. Paul's letters. They are First and Second Corinthians, Galatians, Ephesians, and Philippians. Let us spend a few minutes now noting some of the distinctive features and background of each. *(In this, and in the second program on St. Paul's letters, we have deliberately omitted his Letter to the Romans. The reason for this is that it is so rich in doctrine that it is worthy of special consideration. Consequently, it is our hope that at some future date we will have an entire Peace of Heart program dealing solely with this letter. For the time being, however, much of the essential teaching of Romans can be found in Paul's other letters, especially in Galations.)*

56. We will begin now with an overview of St. Paul's first letter to the Christians at Corinth (I Corinthians).

57. Corinth was the capital of the Roman province of Achaia. Located in Greece, it had been built by the Romans as an outpost on the site of an old Greek city.

58. St. Paul first went to Corinth about A.D. 50 and spent at least a year and a half there. Initially, he gained converts from among the Jewish residents of the city, but the majority remained hostile to him and his work. Later he won adherents to the Faith from among the pagan inhabitants.

59. St. Paul departed from Corinth by the end of 51 and may not have returned for many years. He left his disciple, Apollos, in charge of the fledgling Church, who held it together and also gained new converts from among both Jews and pagans. After about a year he left Corinth to rejoin Paul.

60. Within a year or two of Apollos' departure certain Jewish Christians from Palestine went to Corinth. These had once been zealous missionaries, but were no longer. Falsely claiming to have close ties with the twelve Apostles, they tried to use this boast to undermine St. Paul's work.

61. Apparently these "false apostles," as Paul called them, tolerated an imprudent and dangerous relationship between Corinthian Christians and pagans until serious divisions and gross immorality arose in the Church.

62. As a result of these conditions, a letter was sent to St. Paul by concerned Corinthian Christians describing the situation and asking his advice. About A.D. 56 St. Paul responded, writing his First Letter to the Corinthians. Rich in doctrine, the letter sought to win back the wayward to the true Faith. St. Paul also reprimanded those guilty of various sins, such as incest and drunkeness, and he appealed for funds to aid the Church in Palestine.

II Corinthians

63. A few months after the First Letter to the Corinthians was written, St. Paul wrote again. By this time, however, the troubles affecting the Church in Corinth had somewhat subsided. For example, Second Corinthians tells us that many of those previously misled by the false apostles had returned to the path of Catholic orthodoxy and were again loyal to Paul, the true Apostle.

64. Still, his enemies were not completely silenced. They continued to attack St. Paul by belittling his appearance and speech. They claimed too that he was fickle, and they were outraged that he had turned the Church in Corinth against them.

65. We learn also from Second Corinthians that a man who had contracted an incestuous relationship with his step-mother had been excommunicated, and that St. Paul's plea for aid to the Palestinian Christians had been given a positive response.

66. In general we can say St. Paul wrote his second letter to further the sanctification of the faithful and to confront his adversaries. The predominant spiritual theme of the epistle consists in the fact that good can be found through suffering in union with Christ and His Church.

67.   The Letter to the Galatians was written principally for the pagan or Gentile converts to Christianity who lived in the Roman province of Galatia in Asia Minor. In the letter St. Paul sought to remedy the damage caused by certain perverters of the Faith.

68.   Unlike the false apostles at Corinth, who were lax in doctrinal matters, the enemies in Galatia sought to impose on Gentile Christians burdensome and unnecessary doctrines. Thus they held that pagan converts to Christianity also had to become converts to Judaism and be subject to the entire Old Testament Law of Moses. In essence then, they were saying that mankind was not saved by Christ alone, but also by the Mosaic Law.

69.   St. Paul begins the letter by insisting that the Gospel he preached is from God and that it is complete and unchangeable. He asserts it was revealed to him by Our Lord and, contrary to the claims of his adversaries, it is the same Gospel proclaimed by the other Apostles.

70.   Next, St. Paul dwells at some length on the fact that salvation or justification is received through faith in Christ and not through the Mosaic Law. And he reminds the Galatians that it is through faith in Christ that they received the Holy Spirit. Moreover, it was through faith in God, and in anticipation of Christ's sacrifice on the Cross, that Abraham, the father of the Jewish people,

was saved centuries before the Jews received the Old Testament Law from the hands of Moses.

71.   Paul then insists that the Old Testament Law was not intended to save or justify anyone, rather it served as a guide for knowing God's will until the coming of Christ. It is faith in God, wrote Paul, and not the mere external observance of the Mosaic Law, which brings salvation.

72.   St. Paul concludes this letter by urging the Galatians to forsake the unnecessary observance of the Old Testament Law and to return to supernatural faith in Christ which leads to God's eternal Kingdom.

Ephesians

73.   St. Paul's letter to the Church in Ephesus, located in Asia Minor, was composed while he was in prison — perhaps in Rome. Unlike First and Second Corinthians and Galatians, the Letter to the Ephesians contains no hint of strife. Basically, it is an essay on the unity between Christ and the Church; Christ being the Church's Head. Also the letter reveals God's purpose for the world which is to be accomplished through the Church.

74.   St. Paul writes that through faith and Baptism individuals are united to Christ and to His death on the Cross, so that they may rise through Him and with Him to share in God's life and friendship. Moreover, St. Paul argues that since Christians are members of

Christ, they are members of one another also. He dwells too on ways to maintain and enhance this unity.

75.   Finally, we would like to call your attention to chapter five where St. Paul draws a beautiful comparison between the love Christian spouses should have for one another and the love Our Blessed Lord has for His Church.

Philippians

76.   The Letter to the Philippians was addressed to Christians who lived in Philippi, a city east of Macedonia in what is now northeastern Greece. This letter was also written while St. Paul was in captivity and reveals the deep affection the Apostle had for the Philippian converts. He was especially grateful for the money they gave him during his imprisonment.

77.   While for the most part, the tone of his letter is gentle, St. Paul also passionately warns the Philippians against succumbing to those seeking to enslave them to the Mosaic Law. He also urges them to greater unity among themselves. With respect to doctrine about Christ, the letter has an important and often-quoted section dealing with Our Lord's human and divine natures.

78.   As you meditate on these five letters of St. Paul during the next three weeks, we hope that God will shower you with His blessings, and that you will receive much spiritual fruit.

"Prayers and Recommended Practices"

79. At the end of each of the companion meditations which follow each daily Scripture selection, note the references to Jerry Coniker's "Prayers and Recommended Practices" book. We urge you to obtain a copy and read them. These will give you further insights into the spirituality of the Apostolate for Family Consecration (the Apostolate), including the spirituality of consecration and that of Scripture's Four C's. You will also receive information about the structure of the Apostolate. ("Prayers and Recommended Practices" by Jerome F. Coniker, the Apostolate, Box 220, Kenosha, WI 53141).

Neighborhood Peace of Heart Forums

80. While this book on St. Paul's Letters can be read as a complete unit in itself, it was primarily designed to be a meditation book for one of the Apostolate for Family Consecration's Neighborhood Peace of Heart Forums. Forums conducted by authorized Neighborhood Chapters of the Apostolate. A Peace of Heart Forum consists of four meetings, over a 22-day period, in private homes for small gatherings of neighbors who come together to view the Apostolate's home video tape television programs and participate in discussing the spiritual truths they have read about and meditated on.

81. If you would like to attend a Neighborhood Peace of Heart Forum, or help form a Neighborhood Chapter in your area, please

contact us at the AFC, Box 220, Kenosha, WI 53141.

"Purpose of the Apostolate"

82. The specific purpose of the Apostolate is to utilize programs like this to transform neighborhoods into God-centered communities, communities supportive of the sacredness of family life.

"The Catholic Catechism"
by Fr. John A. Hardon, S.J.

83. You will find many references throughout the following meditations to Father John A. Hardon's "The Catholic Catechism" published by Doubleday and Co., N.Y. This handbook on our Faith is one of the most thorough and concise books of its kind. If you want to get the most out of your meditations, we strongly recommend that you obtain a copy of this book and refer to it as we specify sections from it throughout this text. As Scripture unfolds our Faith, Father Hardon's "The Catholic Catechism" will give you an in-depth knowledge of it in a very quick and easy way. If you wish, you may order a copy from the Apostolate, Box 220, Kenosha, WI 53141.

"Modern Catholic Dictionary"
by Fr. John A. Hardon, S.J.

84. Also referred to in the following meditations are the entries from Fr. Hardon's "Modern Catholic Dictionary," also published by Doubleday and Co. This scholarly work serves as a handy reference book featuring

thousands of short, easy-to-read, entries on religious topics, including those widely mentioned and discussed since the Second Vatican Council. This, too, can be purchased from the Apostolate.

"The Question and Answer Catholic Catechism"
by Fr. John A. Hardon, S.J.

85. Another book by Father Hardon which we strongly recommend for parents to use with their children is "The Question and Answer Catholic Catechism," also published by Doubleday and Co. Completely orthodox and up-to-date, this work is written in the catechetical format familiar to many in parishes and Catholic schools some years ago. One advantage of this catechism over some of the earlier question and answer books is the more complete answers given to the questions. "The Catholic Catechism" and the "Modern Catholic Dictionary" can also be used with this book for supplemental information. "The Question and Answer Catholic Catechism" is available as well from the Apostolate.

1 Corinthians

THE FIRST LETTER
OF PAUL TO THE
CHURCH AT CORINTH

INTRODUCTION

Address and greetings. Thanksgiving

1 1 I, Paul, appointed by God to be an apostle, together with brother Sosthenes, send 2 greetings ·to the church of God in Corinth, to the holy people of Jesus Christ, who are called to take their place among all the saints everywhere who pray to our Lord Jesus Christ; for he is their Lord no less than ours. 3 May God our Father and the Lord Jesus Christ send you grace and peace.

4 I never stop thanking God for all the graces you have received through Jesus 5 Christ. ·I thank him that you have been enriched in so many ways, especially in your 6 teachers and preachers; ·the witness to Christ (C3)

7 has indeed been strong among you •so that you will not be without any of the gifts of the Spirit while you are waiting for our Lord
8 Jesus Christ to be revealed; •and he will keep you steady and without blame until the last (C4)
9 day, the day of our Lord Jesus Christ, •because God by calling you has joined you to his Son, Jesus Christ; and God is faithful.

I. DIVISIONS AND SCANDALS

A. FACTIONS IN THE CORINTHIAN CHURCH

Dissensions among the faithful

10 All the same, I do appeal to you, brothers, for the sake of our Lord Jesus Christ, to make up the differences between you, and instead (C2) of disagreeing among yourselves, to be united again in your belief and practice.
11 From what Chloe's people have been telling me, my dear brothers, it is clear that there are
12 serious differences among you. •What I mean are all these slogans that you have, like: "I (C2) am for Paul," "I am for Apollos," "I am for
13 Cephas,"[a] "I am for Christ." •Has Christ (C2) been parceled out? Was it Paul that was crucified for you? Were you baptized in the name
14 of Paul? •I am thankful that I never baptized
15 any of you after Crispus and Gaius •so none of you can say he was baptized in my name.
16 Then there was the family of Stephanas, of course, that I baptized too, but no one else as far as I can remember.

The true wisdom and the false

17 For Christ did not send me to baptize, but (C3) to preach the Good News, and not to preach that in the terms of philosophy[b] in which the crucifixion of Christ cannot be expressed.
18 The language of the cross may be illogical to

34

those who are not on the way to salvation, but those of us who are on the way see it as 19 God's power to save. •As scripture says: *I shall destroy the wisdom of the wise and bring to nothing all the learning of the learned.* 20 *Where are the philosophers now? Where are the scribes?*[c] Where are any of our thinkers today? Do you see now how God has shown 21 up the foolishness of human wisdom? •If it was God's wisdom that human wisdom should not know God, it was because God wanted to save those who have faith through (C1) the foolishness of the message that we 22 preach. •And so, while the Jews demand miracles and the Greeks look for wisdom, 23 here are we preaching a crucified Christ; to the Jews an obstacle that they cannot get 24 over, to the pagans madness, •but to those who have been called, whether they are Jews or Greeks, a Christ who is the power and the 25 wisdom of God. •For God's foolishness is wiser than human wisdom, and God's weakness is stronger than human strength.

26 Take yourselves for instance, brothers, at the time when you were called: how many of you were wise in the ordinary sense of the word, how many were influential people, or 27 came from noble families? •No, it was to shame the wise that God chose what is foolish by human reckoning, and to shame what is strong that he chose what is weak by hu-28 man reckoning; •those whom the world thinks common and contemptible are the ones that God has chosen—those who are (C2) nothing at all to show up those who are ev-29 erything. •The human race has nothing to 30 boast about to God, •but you God has made (C2) members of Christ Jesus and by God's doing he has become our wisdom, and our virtue, 31 and our holiness, and our freedom. •As scripture says: *if anyone wants to boast, let him boast about the Lord.*[d]

1 **2** As for me, brothers, when I came to you, it was not with any show of oratory or philosophy, but simply to tell you what God (C3)
2 had guaranteed. ·During my stay with you, the only knowledge I claimed to have was about Jesus, and only about him as the cruci-
3 fied Christ. ·Far from relying on any power of my own, I came among you in great "fear
4 and trembling"[a] ·and in my speeches and the sermons that I gave, there were none of the arguments that belong to philosophy; only a (C3)
demonstration of the power of the Spirit. (C1)
5 And I did this so that your faith should not depend on human philosophy but on the power of God.
6 But still we have a wisdom to offer those who have reached maturity: not a philosophy of our age, it is true, still less of the masters of our age, which are coming to their end.

7 The hidden wisdom of God which we teach in our mysteries is the wisdom that God predestined to be for our glory before the
8 ages began. ·It is a wisdom that none of the masters of this age have ever known, or they would not have crucified the Lord of Glory;
9 we teach what scripture calls: *the things that no eye has seen and no ear has heard, things* (C3) *beyond the mind of man, all that God has prepared for those who love him.*[b]

10 These are the very things that God has
revealed to us through the Spirit, for the
Spirit reaches the depths of everything, even
11 the depths of God. •After all, the depths of
a man can only be known by his own spirit,
not by any other man, and in the same way
the depths of God can only be known by the
12 Spirit of God. •Now instead of the spirit of
the world, we have received the Spirit that
comes from God, to teach us to understand
13 the gifts that he has given us. •Therefore we (C3)
teach, not in the way in which philosophy is
taught, but in the way that the Spirit teaches

14 us: we teach spiritual things spiritually. •An
unspiritual person is one who does not accept (C2)
anything of the Spirit of God: he sees it all
as nonsense; it is beyond his understanding
because it can only be understood by means (C2)
15 of the Spirit. •A spiritual man, on the other (C1)
hand, is able to judge the value of everything, (C2)
and his own value is not to be judged by other
16 men. •As scripture says: *Who can know the* (C3)
mind of the Lord, so who can teach him?[c] But
we are those who have the mind of Christ.

3 ¹ Brothers, I myself was unable to speak to you as people of the Spirit: I treated you _(C2) ² as sensual men, still infants in Christ. •What _(C3) I fed you with was milk, not solid food, for you were not ready for it; and indeed, you are _(C2) ³ still not ready for it •since you are still un-spiritual. Isn't that obvious from all the jeal-ousy and wrangling that there is among you, _(C2) from the way that you go on behaving like ⁴ ordinary people? •What could be more un- _(C2) spiritual than your slogans, "I am for Paul" and "I am for Apollos"?

The place of the Christian preacher

⁵ After all, what is Apollos and what is Paul? They are servants who brought the faith to _(C3) you. Even the different ways in which they brought it were assigned to them by the Lord. ⁶ I did the planting, Apollos did the watering, _(C3) ⁷ but God made things grow. •Neither the _(C3) planter nor the waterer matters: only God, ⁸ who makes things grow. •It is all one who _(C3) does the planting and who does the watering, and each will duly be paid according to his ⁹ share in the work. •We are fellow workers with God; you are God's farm, God's build- _(C3) ing.

¹⁰ By the grace God gave me, I succeeded _(C3) as an architect and laid the foundations, on which someone else is doing the building. Everyone doing the building must work care- _(C3) ¹¹ fully. •For the foundation, nobody can lay any other than the one which has already been ¹² laid, that is Jesus Christ. •On this foundation you can build in gold, silver and jewels, or ¹³ in wood, grass and straw, •but whatever the material, the work of each builder is going to _(C3) be clearly revealed when the day comes. That day will begin with fire, and the fire will test ¹⁴ the quality of each man's work. •If his struc-ture stands up to it, he will get his wages; ¹⁵ if it is burned down, he will be the loser, and _(C2) though he is saved himself, it will be as one

38

who has gone through fire.

16 Didn't you realize that you were God's temple and that the Spirit of God was living
17 among you? ·If anybody should destroy the temple of God, God will destroy him, because the temple of God is sacred; and you (C2) are that temple.

Conclusions

18 Make no mistake about it: if any one of you thinks of himself as wise, in the ordinary sense of the word, then he must learn to be (C1)
19 a fool before he really can be wise. ·Why? (C2) Because the wisdom of this world is foolishness to God. As scripture says: *The Lord knows wise men's thoughts: he knows how* (C3)
20 *useless they are:ᵃ* ·or again: *God is not con-*
21 *vinced by the arguments of the wise.ᵇ* ·So there is nothing to boast about in anything
22 human: Paul, Apollos, Cephas, the world, life and death, the present and the future, are
23 all your servants; ·but you belong to Christ and Christ belongs to God.

Week 1 Day 1
Four C's Meditations
on 1 Corinthians 1:1-3:23

1. Lord Jesus, we now begin a series of meditations on the writings of your Apostle, St. Paul. He was truly a man for his times. His continual trust in You and his constant charity motivated him to endure years of unrelenting hardships so he could gain thousands of souls for Your eternal Kingdom. *(Be sure to read the introductory remarks on this letter found in paragraphs 57-62 of the Introduction to this book.)*

2. In his own words, St. Paul tells us a portion of what he gladly suffered so others might share in the joy and peace he derived from loving and confiding in You.

3. "But if anyone wants some brazen speaking — I am still talking as a fool — then I can be as brazen as any of them, and about the same things. Hebrews, are they? So am I. Israelites? So am I. Descendants of Abraham? So am I. The servants of Christ? I must be mad to say this, but so am I, and more than they: more, because I have worked harder, I have been sent to prison more often, and whipped so many times more, often almost to death. Five times I had the thirty-nine lashes from the Jews; three times I have been beaten with sticks; once I was stoned; three times I have been shipwrecked and once adrift in the open sea for a night and a day. Constantly traveling, I have been in danger from rivers and in danger from brigands, in danger from my own people and in danger from pagans;

in danger in the towns, in danger in the open country, danger at sea and danger from so-called brothers. I have worked and labored, often without sleep; I have been hungry and thirsty and often starving; I have been in the cold without clothes. And, to leave out much more, there is my daily preoccupation: my anxiety for all the churches."[1] *The number (1) refers to the Scripture references found beginning on p. 243*

4. Lord, if anyone ever followed in Your footsteps it was St. Paul. Yet, this was the same man who prior to becoming a Christian, persecuted Your followers and delivered many to their deaths.[2]

5. Merciful Savior, we see amply reflected throughout the two letters to the Corinthians, St. Paul's sacrificial love for his spiritual children, the members of the Corinthian Church. Even his sternness towards some of them was motivated by charity, since it was exercised with the intent of bringing them back to the path of salvation.

6. In the following passage we get a glimpse of the affectionate side of his love for those in Corinth.

7. "By my life, I call God to witness that the reason why I did not come to Corinth after all was to spare your feelings. We are not dictators over your faith, but are fellow workers with you for your happiness; in the faith you are steady enough. Well then, I made up my mind not to pay you a second

41

distressing visit. I may have hurt you, but if so I have hurt the only people who could give me any pleasure. I wrote as I did to make sure that, when I came, I should not be distressed by the very people who should have made me happy. I am sure you all know that I could never be happy unless you were. When I wrote to you, in deep distress and anguish of mind, and in tears, it was not to make you feel hurt but to let you know how much love I have for you."[3]

8. Jesus, help parents to follow in St. Paul's footsteps so they may always be concerned for the spiritual welfare of their children. By word and example may they teach them what it means to be Your disciples. Inspire parents to make adequate provisions for their children's religious education, both at home and in school. And help them to lead their families properly in prayer, and to encourage each member to love You in every person that comes into their lives. Moreover, may they never forget to pray for their families daily.

9.   Lord, we noticed in today's Scripture reading that the Church at Corinth was split into various factions. Thus the good You had accomplished through Paul and his companions was being destroyed. Consequently, Paul appealed to the Corinthians to eliminate their divisions by adhering to Your teaching.

10.   Yes, Jesus, every church should be free of divisiveness, whether it is a regional church, the diocesan church, the parish church, or the domestic church consisting of parents and children. When divisiveness occurs, the only beneficiaries are the powers of darkness. Help us always exercise mutual seed-charity and unite us in the Faith You entrusted to the safekeeping of the Catholic Church. Also, since our pastors are our spiritual fathers, continually remind us to pray for them and support them in their work. May they always remain faithful to their priestly vocation.

11.   Most Sacred Heart of Jesus, St. Paul reminds us that many regard the Faith as foolishness.[4] How then can we win them over to You? Sophisticated arguments demonstrating the reasonableness of the Faith may not convince many. Moreover, some of us are not capable of approaching people in this manner. But we can all attract others to You by being faithful to Your teaching and by loving You in our neighbor. God-centered lives draw like magnets those who are sincerely seeking religious truth. Jesus, may we always be inspired by Your Holy Spirit to

lead saintly lives so we may attract many to Your Kingdom.

12.   Finally, Lord, our attention focused on St. Paul's comparison between a Christian community's apostolic work and the labor of workmen putting up a building.[5] The labor of some, he says, is like building with gold, silver and jewels; while that of others is like working with wood, grass and straw. Presumably, the wood, grass, and straw represent an inferior exercise of self-sacrificing love. Yet, since they remain in Your friendship they will be saved, but not without some punishment for the poorer quality of their Christian lives.

13. Again, Lord, may Your Holy Spirit continually inspire us to lead God-centered lives. May our labor in the world be solidly based on Your will. Especially may we labor with the precious metals and stones of sacrificial good works, whereby we build up Your Church, avoid the pains of hell and, hopefully, the fires of Purgatory as well. Amen.

(See Father Hardon's "The Catholic Catechism," Doubleday, N.Y., pp. 273-280 for a discussion of Purgatory. This book may be purchased from The Apostolate, Box 220, Kenosha, WI 53141.)

Try to read these Scripture passages and meditations several times a day in a reflective manner. Each time you do so, the Holy Spirit will give you more insights.
Please read the Foreword by Dale Francis and the prayer immediately preceding it in our "Prayers and Recommended Practices" prayer book.

1 **4** People must think of us as Christ's servants, stewards entrusted with the myster-
2 ies of God. •What is expected of stewards is
that each one should be found worthy of his
3 trust. •Not that it makes the slightest differ- (C1)
ence to me whether you, or indeed any hu-
man tribunal, find me worthy or not. I will
4 not even pass judgment on myself. •True, my (C2)
conscience does not reproach me at all, but
that does not prove that I am acquitted: the
5 Lord alone is my judge. •There must be no
passing of premature judgment. Leave that (C2)
until the Lord comes: he will light up all that
is hidden in the dark and reveal the secret (C2)
intentions of men's hearts. Then will be the
time for each one to have whatever praise he
deserves, from God.

6 Now in everything I have said here, brothers, I have taken Apollos and myself as an
example (remember the maxim: "Keep to (C2)
what is written"); it is not for you, so full of
your own importance, to go taking sides for
7 one man against another. •In any case,
brother, has anybody given you some special
right? What do you have that was not given
to you? And if it was given, how can you
8 boast as though it were not? •Is it that you (C2)

have everything you want—that you are rich
already, in possession of your kingdom, with
us left outside? Indeed I wish you were really
9 kings, and we could be kings with you! •But
instead, it seems to me, God has put us apostles at the end of his parade, with the men (C2)
sentenced to death; it is true—we have been
put on show in front of the whole universe,
10 angels as well as men. •Here we are, fools (C3)
for the sake of Christ, while you are the
learned men in Christ; we have no power, but
you are influential; you are celebrities, we are

11 nobodies. ·To this day, we go without food (C3)
and drink and clothes; we are beaten and have (C2)
12 no homes; ·we work for our living with our (C3)
own hands. When we are cursed, we answer (C2)
with a blessing; when we are hounded, we
13 put up with it; ·we are insulted and we an- (C3)
swer politely. We are treated as the offal (C2)
of the world, still to this day, the scum of the (C2)
earth.

An appeal

14 I am saying all this not just to make you (C3)
ashamed but to bring you, as my dearest chil-
15 dren, to your senses. ·You might have thousands of guardians in Christ, but not more
than one father and it was I who begot you
in Christ Jesus by preaching the Good News.
16 17 That is why I beg you to copy me ·and why (C3)
I have sent you Timothy, my dear and faithful (C1)
son in the Lord: he will remind you of the
way that I live in Christ, as I teach it every- (C3)
where in all the churches.

18 When it seemed that I was not coming to
visit you, some of you became self-important, (C2)
19 but I will be visiting you soon, the Lord willing, and then I shall want to know not what
these self-important people have to say, but (C2)
20 what they can do, ·since the kingdom of God
21 is not just words, it is power. ·It is for you (C3)
to decide: do I come with a stick in my hand
or in a spirit of love and goodwill?

B. INCEST IN CORINTH

1 **5** I have been told as an undoubted fact that
one of you is living with his father's wife.*a* (C2)
This is a case of sexual immorality among (C2)
you that must be unparalleled even among
2 pagans. ·How can you be proud of yourselves? You should be in mourning. A man (C2)
who does a thing like that ought to have been (C3)
3 expelled from the community. ·Though I am (C3)

47

far away in body, I am with you in spirit, and (C3)
have already condemned the man who did
4 this thing as if I were actually present. •When (C2)
you are assembled together in the name of (C1)
the Lord Jesus, and I am spiritually present
with you, then with the power of our Lord
5 Jesus •he is to be handed over to Satan so that (C3)
his sensual body may be destroyed and his
spirit saved on the day of the Lord.

6   The pride that you take in yourselves is (C2)
hardly to your credit. You must know how
even a small amount of yeast is enough to
7 leaven all the dough, •so get rid of all the old (C2)
yeast, and make yourselves into a completely
new batch of bread, unleavened as you are (C3)
meant to be. Christ, our Passover, has been
8 sacrificed; •let us celebrate the feast, then, by (C2)
getting rid of all the old yeast of evil and
wickedness, having only the unleavened (C3)
bread of sincerity and truth.*b*

9   When I wrote in my letter to you not to
associate with people living immoral lives, (C2)

10 I was not meaning to include all the people (C2)
in the world who are sexually immoral, any
more than I meant to include all usurers and (C2)
swindlers or idol-worshipers. To do that, you
would have to withdraw from the world alto-

11 gether. •What I wrote was that you should not
   associate with a brother Christian who is
   leading an immoral life, or is a usurer, or (C2)
   idolatrous, or a slanderer, or a drunkard, or
   is dishonest; you should not even eat a meal (C2)
12 with people like that. •It is not my business
   to pass judgment on those outside. Of those
   who are inside, you can surely be the judges.
13 But of those who are outside, God is the
   judge.

   *You must drive out this evil-doer from
   among you.*[c]

Week 1 Day 2
Four C's Meditations
on 1 Corinthians 4:1-5:13

1. At the beginning of today's Scripture
reading, Most Merciful Savior, St. Paul drew
attention to the fact that he, Peter, and their
fellow-worker, Apollos, were Your stewards.
As such, they were entrusted with the
mysteries of God. That is, they were
entrusted with things up to then hidden, but
from then on were to be revealed to the world
through Your Church. As Your stewards,

You expected them to reveal the mystery of Your saving doctrine, and to dispense Your holy sacraments with perseverance and a deep love for souls.

2. We, too, because we are Christians are Your stewards. And as such You have called us laymen to reveal to others the Good News of salvation. By exercising this stewardship, we extend and build up Your Church, which is the Kingdom of God on earth. *(See "The Catholic Catechism," p. 209, for some words on God's Kingdom.)*

3. As Your stewards, we must remain faithful. Yet, Lord, this is impossible without the continual assistance of Your grace. Inspire us to pray daily with fervor, and encourage us to attend Mass often, so that we may obtain the graces necessary for the tasks You have given us. Let us rely not on our strength but on You Who are the Source of all grace.

4. Most Sacred Heart of Jesus, there are so many people who do not know You. Consequently, they have not experienced Your charity and peace in their hearts. How selfish of us, how lacking in seed-charity, if we make no attempts to share You with them. We would be like the unworthy servant who refused to use his talent and buried it in the ground.[6]

5. To be honest, Lord, we are often afraid to approach others with the Good news about You and salvation. We sometimes fear we will be laughed at and rejected, or that we might be imposing ourselves on others. Nonethe-

less, we should be willing to take the risk of ridicule and rejection. And certainly, anyone who has good news to share with others should not feel he would be imposing on them. We need only reflect on what You suffered for us, and on what St. Paul suffered for the sake of Your Name, in order to be ashamed of ourselves even for hesitating to share You with others.

6.   There may indeed be some who would reject us, but there undoubtedly would be many others who would gratefully accept our efforts on their behalf. And as You have already touched the hearts of millions through the work of Your servants in the past, You will reach even more through our own efforts.

7.   Yes, Lord, there are members of our own families and some of our friends and co-workers who, to the best of our knowledge, have not yet accepted You and Your doctrine. Give us the courage to approach them, and illuminate our minds so we will use the right words and the correct means to bring them to You.

8.   Surely, Lord, the first few attempts will be the hardest. But like other things in life, once we get started and repeat our efforts, things will become easier and we will probably find that most of our fears were ill-founded. And, of course, we know that when we sacrifice ourselves for others in this manner You will be with us even to the end of time. [7]

9.   Further on in our reading, Jesus, St. Paul

51

speaks of those Corinthian Christians who were filled with an inflated sense of self-importance.[8] Actually, this attitude reflected the sin of pride or self-centeredness which leads to all other sins.

10.   When we fall into the sin of pride, we tend to think of ourselves as the center of the universe. In effect, we tend to think of ourselves as if we were God and that the universe revolved around us. The direct opposite of this sin is the virtue of supernatural seed-charity or self-sacrifice for You, Lord, and for our neighbor. When we begin to exercise this gift we become increasingly God-centered, not self-centered. We also receive the grace of humility whereby we see ourselves as You see us. We see ourselves, then, not as the center of the universe, but as Your instruments who are dependent on You Who are the true center of the universe and the Source of all our natural and supernatural gifts, including the gift of our salvation. St. Paul rightly wrote, "What do you have that was not given to you? And if it was given, how can you boast as if it were not?"[9]

11. Unfortunately, Lord, there are times when we deceive ourselves into thinking we are the source of all our attributes. We take pride in this talent or that as if we had created them. We too often fail to reflect on the fact that all the good we have comes from You either directly or indirectly. And at times, we also fail to reflect on the fact that we do not always use our talents properly.

12. Dear Lord, constantly supply us with the gift of seed-charity so we can sacrifice ourselves for You Who are the true center of the universe and the Source of all that is good. And Jesus, grant that we may be willing to suffer, if necessary, even as You and St. Paul did for the sake of bringing others into Your Kingdom. Help us to keep in mind, too, that the faithful fulfillment of our responsibilities and the offering up of our trials can repair for sin and bring us much closer to You.

13. St. Paul also mentioned in today's reading the Christian who defiled his conscience by having an incestuous relationship with his step-mother. St. Paul was equally displeased with the faithful for neglecting to discipline the offender. Thus, he ordered that the culprit be "handed over to satan," i.e., to be excommunicated so he might eventually be saved. [10]

14. Actually the man, because of his grave sin, was already living in satan's kingdom of darkness. And since he was unrepentant there was no valid reason why he should enjoy the benefits of those who were leading lives of seed-charity. Moreover, his scandalous conduct was setting a bad example for all.

15. St. Paul hoped, of course, that in the process of being exiled from the Christian community, the sinner, eventually experiencing the bitter fruit of his sin, would repent and be received back with joy into the full fellowship of the Church.

16. We see in this incident, Lord, how discipline can also be an act of seed-charity. By disciplining the sinner with excommunication, St. Paul desired to obtain his salvation and to protect the faithful from the example of scandalous conduct.

17. Jesus, Our Lord and Master, Christian parents must, from time to time, exercise discipline over the community known as the Christian family. Grant them the courage to

discipline their children when they need it, but may it always be done in the spirit of Christian love. Help parents realize that undisciplined children will inevitably become self-centered, spoiled children, lacking unselfish generosity, thus alienating themselves from You, the Source of all charity, goodness and happiness.

18.   We also noted in our meditations, Lord, St. Paul's important instruction regarding the attitude of Christians towards non-Christians leading immoral lives.[11] He pointed out that Christians should not entirely avoid such persons. The reason being, not that their conduct should be condoned, but that through the missionary zeal of the Christian community they might be brought, in repentance, to You and Your Kingdom. As You said, "I did not come to call the virtuous, but sinners."[12] You also said through St. Paul that we Christians were to live in the world, but not as part of the world.[13]

19.   Lord grant that we through Your grace may overcome the temptations of the world, the flesh and the devil, and may we win many souls for Your Kingdom. Amen.

Try to read these Scripture passages and meditations in a reflective manner every day. The Holy Spirit will reveal more insights to you each time you do so.

Please read the Preface in our "Prayers and Recommended Practices" book.

WEEK 1 DAY 3
1 Corinthians 6:1-7:40

C. RECOURSE TO THE PAGAN COURTS

1 **6** How dare one of your members take up   (C2)
a complaint against another in the law-
courts of the unjust*a* instead of before the
2 saints? •As you know, it is the saints who are
to "judge the world"; and if the world is to

be judged by you, how can you be unfit to
3 judge trifling cases? •Since we are also to
judge angels, it follows that we can judge
4 matters of everyday life; •but when you have
had cases of that kind, the people you appointed to try them were not even respected
5 in the Church. •You should be ashamed: is
there really not one reliable man among you
6 to settle differences between brothers •and so
one brother brings a court case against an-
7 other in front of unbelievers? •It is bad   (C2)
enough for you to have lawsuits at all against
one another: oughtn't you to let yourselves
be wronged, and let yourselves be cheated?   (C3)
8 But you are doing the wronging and the
cheating, and to your own brothers.   (C2)

56

9   You know perfectly well that people who
     do wrong will not inherit the kingdom of (c2)
     God: people of immoral lives, idolaters, adul- (c2)
10 terers, catamites, sodomites. •thieves, usu-
     rers, drunkards, slanderers and swindlers will
11 never inherit the kingdom of God. •These are
     the sort of people some of you were once, (c2)
     but now you have been washed clean, and
     sanctified, and justified through the name of
     the Lord Jesus Christ and through the Spirit
     of our God.

D. FORNICATION [r]

12   "For me there are no forbidden things"; [b]
     maybe, but not everything does good. I agree
     there are no forbidden things for me, but I
     am not going to let anything dominate me.
13 Food is only meant for the stomach, and the
     stomach for food; yes, and God is going to
     do away with both of them. But the body— (c2)
     this is not meant for fornication; it is for the
14 Lord, and the Lord for the body. •God, who
     raised the Lord from the dead, will by his
     power raise us up too.
15   You know, surely, that your bodies are
     members making up the body of Christ; do
     you think I can take parts of Christ's body (c2)
     and join them to the body of a prostitute?
16 Never! •As you know, a man who goes with (c2)
     a prostitute is one body with her, since *the*
17 *two,* as it is said, *become one flesh.* •But any- (c3)
     one who is joined to the Lord is one spirit
     with him.
18   Keep away from fornication. All the other (c2)
     sins are committed outside the body; but to
     fornicate is to sin against your own body.
19 Your body, you know, is the temple of the (c2)
     Holy Spirit, who is in you since you received
     him from God. You are not your own prop-
20 erty; •you have been bought and paid for. (c3)
     That is why you should use your body for the (c3)
     glory of God.

II. ANSWERS TO VARIOUS QUESTIONS

A. MARRIAGE AND VIRGINITY

1 **7** Now for the questions about which you wrote. Yes, it is a good thing for a man 2 not to touch a woman; ·but since sex is always a danger, let each man have his own wife and 3 each woman her own husband. ·The husband must give his wife what she has the right to (C3) expect, and so too the wife to the husband. 4 The wife has no rights over her own body; it is the husband who has them. In the same way, the husband has no rights over his body; 5 the wife has them. ·Do not refuse each other (C2) except by mutual consent, and then only for (C3) an agreed time, to leave yourselves free for prayer; then come together again in case Satan should take advantage of your weakness (C2) 6 to tempt you. ·This is a suggestion, not a rule: 7 I should like everyone to be like me, but everybody has his own particular gifts from God, one with a gift for one thing and another with a gift for the opposite.

8 There is something I want to add for the sake of widows and those who are not married: it is a good thing for them to stay as they (C3)

9 are, like me, •but if they cannot control the
sexual urges, they should get married, since (C2)
it is better to be married than to be tortured.

10   For the married I have something to say,
and this is not from me but from the Lord: (C2)

11 a wife must not leave her husband—•or if she
does leave him, she must either remain un- (C3)
married or else make it up with her husband—nor must a husband send his wife (C2)
away.

12   The rest is from me and not from the Lord.
If a brother has a wife who is an unbeliever,
and she is content to live with him, he must (C2)

13 not send her away; •and if a woman has an
unbeliever for her husband, and he is content

14 to live with her, she must not leave him. •This (C2)
is because the unbelieving husband is made
one with the saints through his wife, and the
unbelieving wife is made one with the saints
through her husband. If this were not so,
your children would be unclean, whereas in

15 fact they are holy. •However, if the unbelieving partner does not consent, they may separate; in these circumstances, the brother or
sister is not tied: God has called you to a life (C3)

16 of peace. •If you are a wife, it may be your (C3)
part to save your husband, for all you know;
if a husband, for all you know, it may be your (C3)
part to save your wife.

17 For the rest, what each one has is what the Lord has given him and he should continue as he was when God's call reached him. This is the ruling that I give in all the churches.
18 If anyone had already been circumcised at the time of his call, he need not disguise it, and anyone who was uncircumcised at the time
19 of his call need not be circumcised; ·because to be circumcised or uncircumcised means nothing: what does matter is to keep (C3)
20 the commandments of God. ·Let everyone
21 stay as he was at the time of his call. ·If, when you were called, you were a slave, do not let this bother you; but if you should have the
22 chance of being free, accept it. ·A slave, when he is called in the Lord, becomes the (C1) Lord's freedman, and a freeman called in the (C3)
23 Lord becomes Christ's slave. ·You have all been bought and paid for; do not be slaves (C2,
24 of other men. ·Each one of you, my brothers, should stay as he was before God at the time of his call.
25 About remaining celibate, I have no directions from the Lord but give my own opinion as one who, by the Lord's mercy, has stayed (C4)
26 faithful. ·Well then, I believe that in these present times of stress this is right: that it is
27 good for a man to stay as he is. ·If you are (C2) tied to a wife, do not look for freedom; if you are free of a wife, then do not look for one.
28 But if you marry, it is no sin, and it is not a sin for a young girl to get married. They will have their troubles, though, in their married life, and I should like to spare you that.
29 Brothers, this is what I mean: our time is growing short. Those who have wives should
30 live as though they had none, ·and those who mourn should live as though they had nothing to mourn for; those who are enjoying life should live as though there were nothing to laugh about; those whose life is buying things should live as though they had nothing of
31 their own; ·and those who have to deal with

60

the world should not become engrossed in (C2)
it. I say this because the world as we know
it is passing away.

32   I would like to see you free from all worry.
An unmarried man can devote himself to the
Lord's affairs, all he need worry about is (C3)
33 pleasing the Lord; ·but a married man has to
bother about the world's affairs and devote
34 himself to pleasing his wife: ·he is torn two (C3)
ways. In the same way an unmarried woman,
like a young girl, can devote herself to the
Lord's affairs; all she need worry about is (C3)
being holy in body and spirit. The married (C2)
woman, on the other hand, has to worry (C3)
about the world's affairs and devote herself
35 to pleasing her husband. ·I say this only to
help you, not to put a halter round your (C3)
necks, but simply to make sure that everything is as it should be, and that you give your
undivided attention to the Lord. (C3)

36   Still, if there is anyone who feels that it
would not be fair to his daughter to let her
grow too old for marriage, and that he should
do something about it, he is free to do as he
likes: he is not sinning if there is a marriage.
37 On the other hand, if someone has firmly
made his mind up, without any compulsion
and in complete freedom of choice, to keep
his daughter as she is, he will be doing a good
38 thing. ·In other words, the man who sees that
his daughter is married has done a good thing (C3)
but the man who keeps his daughter unmar- (C3)
ried has done something even better.[a]

39   A wife is tied as long as her husband is
alive. But if the husband dies, she is free to
marry anybody she likes, only it must be in
40 the Lord. ·She would be happier, in my opinion, if she stayed as she is—and I too have
the Spirit of God, I think.

Week 1 Day 3
Four C's Meditations
on 1 Corinthians 6:1-7:40

1. Today, Jesus, in reading Sacred Scripture we realized a truth about our fallen human nature. We became conscious of the fact that humans generations ago were just as prone to sins of the flesh as they are today. The problems within the Corinthian Church of the first century clearly demonstrated this truth.

2. Some in the Corinthian Church apparently had twisted St. Paul's teaching in order to justify immoral sexual conduct. Indeed, he did say that for him there were no forbidden things, meaning perhaps, there were no righteous things forbidden him.[14] But, whatever he meant, he did not mean he could do anything whatsoever (including the practice of mortal sin) and still remain in the state of grace and in friendship with You. This is made clear when he said that adulterers, homosexuals, drunkards, and others, lacking

pure consciences, were barred from the Kingdom of Heaven.[15] On the other hand, St. Paul was not declaring that these sinners could never inherit Heaven, but only if they refused to repent.

3. Also, judging from today's reading, it appears some Corinthian Christians had incorrectly argued as some people do today that just as the body needs food for sustenance, so the body needs sexual activity. This is contrary to the truth. Thousands of dedicated Religious, and other single people have over the centuries proven that sexual conduct is not necessary for a happy and joyful human life. Who could seriously claim, for example, that prostitutes or practicing homosexuals are happier than, or as happy as, those saintly Religious and other singles who have completely abstained from sexual conduct for the sake of Your Kingdom?

4. St. Paul echoed Your teaching in St. Matthew's Gospel, Lord, when he spoke about fornication. He said that this particular sin is a sin not only against You but against our own bodies, since they are meant to be temples of the Holy Spirit.[16]

5. Jesus, Our Lord, temptations to commit sexual sins and other sins of the flesh are very prevalent today, both among the married and unmarried. And for many of us they are very hard to resist. Yet thankfully, You have promised that with every temptation You would provide a way of escape. You also said You would not allow us to be tempted

beyond our endurance.[(17)] Lord, may we take comfort in these words and remain constant in our endeavors to conquer temptations. By constantly trying, we demonstrate as well the virtues of confidence and seed-charity.

6. Lord, we are also reminded of the testimony of the saints to the effect that Your Blessed Mother will provide great assistance if we call upon her when we are tempted to sin against purity. She who loves us poor sinners so much will not leave us defenseless. The words of the "Memorare," for example, attest to the power of her intercession.

7. "Remember, O Most Gracious Virgin Mary, that never was it known that anyone who fled to your protection, implored your help or sought your intercession was left unaided. Inspired with this confidence, I fly to you, O Virgin of virgins, my Mother. To you I come, before you I stand, sinful and sorrowful. Mother of the Word Incarnate, do not ignore my petitions but in your mercy hear and answer me."

8. Next, Lord, St. Paul teaches that Your gift of sex, which is reserved exclusively for marriage, is to be used unselfishly. Each spouse is to give of himself or herself for the benefit of the other.[18] Moreover, the wife has the exclusive right to the use of her husband's body, and the husband has the exclusive right to his wife's body.[19] Jesus, help married couples to sacrifice themselves constantly for the benefit of their spouses, knowing that in doing so they will draw even closer to You and to a life of sanctity.

9. Finally, Lord, we focused on St. Paul's discussion on the celibate or single state.[20] He holds, as does Your Church, that celibacy consecrated to Your service is a more excellent state than that of marriage, and he gives practical reasons for stating so. Anyone who reads his words carefully will see that, contrary to what some believe, he in no way holds that marriage is evil or that it is not conducive to sanctity. In essence, he simply points out that the single person is able to give more of his or her undivided attention to You. Anyone who is married, especially with a house full of children, should find no difficulty in agreeing with that.

10. The fact is, Lord, most people do marry and it is comforting to know that sacramental marriage is a means of sanctification. Certainly, it is a challenging vocation and most couples find marriage filled with both rewards and hardships. *(See Austin Flannery, O.P. (ed.) "Vatican Council II," pp. 950-952, for a presentation on the Church's teaching on the sanctity of marriage.)*

11. Jesus, Mary and Joseph, you are the model of a perfect and holy family. We ask you in humility and charity to help all family members to be more charitable and patient with one another's faults. May parents, for instance, become constant examples of unselfish love for one another and for their children, and may children, following the good examples of their parents, find peace and happiness in their hearts through obedience and unrelenting sacrificial love. Amen.

Try to re-read and re-meditate on these Scripture passages and meditations at least one more time today. Please read and meditate on Chapter I, Paragraphs 1 to 28 in our "Prayers and Recommended Practices" book.

WEEK 1 DAY 4
1 Corinthians 8:1-9:27

B. FOOD OFFERED TO IDOLS

General principles

1 **8** Now about food sacrificed to idols. "We
all have knowledge"; yes, that is so, but
knowledge gives self-importance—it is love (C2)
2 that makes the building grow. •A man may (C3)

imagine he understands something, but still
not understand anything in the way that he
3 ought to. •But any man who loves God is (C3)
4 known by him. •Well then, about eating food
sacrificed to idols:*a* we know that idols do not
really exist in the world and that there is no
5 god but the One. •And even if there were
things called gods, either in the sky or on
earth—where there certainly seem to be
6 "gods" and "lords" in plenty—•still for us
there is one God, the Father, from whom all
things come and for whom we exist; and
there is one Lord, Jesus Christ, through
whom all things come and through whom we
exist.

7   Some people, however, do not have this
knowledge. There are some who have been
so long used to idols that they eat this food
as though it really had been sacrificed to the
idol, and their conscience, being weak, is
8 defiled by it. •Food, of course, cannot bring   (C2)
us in touch with God: we lose nothing if we
9 refuse to eat, we gain nothing if we eat. •Only
be careful that you do not make use of this
freedom in a way that proves a pitfall for the   (C2)
10 weak. •Suppose someone sees you, a man
who understands, eating in some temple of
an idol; his own conscience, even if it is weak,
may encourage him to eat food which has   (C2)
11 been offered to idols. •In this way your
knowledge could become the ruin of some-   (C2)
one weak, of a brother for whom Christ died.
12 By sinning in this way against your brothers,
and injuring their weak consciences, it would
13 be Christ against whom you sinned. •That is   (C2)
why, since food can be the occasion of my   (C3)
brother's downfall, I shall never eat meat
again in case I am the cause of a brother's
downfall.   (C2)

Paul invokes his own example

1 9I, personally, am free: I am an apostle and
I have seen Jesus our Lord. You are all
2 my work in the Lord. •Even if I were not an
apostle to others, I should still be an apostle
to you who are the seal of my apostolate in
3 the Lord. •My answer to those who want to
4 interrogate me is this: •Have we not every
5 right to eat and drink?*a* •And the right to take
a Christian woman round with us, like all the
other apostles and the brothers of the Lord
6 and Cephas? •Are Barnabas and I the only
ones who are not allowed to stop working?
7 Nobody ever paid money to stay in the army,
and nobody ever planted a vineyard and
refused to eat the fruit of it. Who has there

ever been that kept a flock and did not feed
on the milk from his flock?

8 These may be only human comparisons,
but does not the Law itself say the same
9 thing? ·It is written in the Law of Moses: *You
must not put a muzzle on the ox when it is
treading out the corn.*[b] Is it about oxen that
10 God is concerned, ·or is there not an obvious
reference to ourselves? Clearly this was written for our sake to show that the plowman
ought to plow in expectation, and the
thresher to thresh in the expectation of get-
11 ting his share. ·If we have sown spiritual
things for you, why should you be surprised
12 if we harvest your material things? ·Others (c3)
are allowed these rights over you and our
right is surely greater? In fact we have never (c3)
exercised this right. On the contrary we have (c3)
put up with anything rather than obstruct the
13 Good News of Christ in any way. ·Remem- (c2)
ber that the ministers serving in the Temple
get their food from the Temple and those
serving at the altar can claim their share from
14 the altar itself. ·In the same sort of way the
Lord directed that those who preach the gospel should get their living from the gospel.
15 However, I have not exercised any of these (c3)
rights, and I am not writing all this to secure
this treatment for myself. I would rather die
than let anyone take away something that I
16 can boast of. ·Not that I do boast of preaching
the gospel, since it is a duty which has been (c3)
laid on me; I should be punished if I did not (c2)
17 preach it! ·If I had chosen this work myself,
I might have been paid for it, but as I have
not, it is a responsibility which has been put
18 into my hands. ·Do you know what my reward is? It is this: in my preaching, to be able
to offer the Good News free, and not insist (c3)
on the rights which the gospel gives me.
19 So though I am not a slave of any man I
have made myself the slave of everyone so
20 as to win as many as I could. ·I made myself (c3)

a Jew to the Jews, to win the Jews; that is,
I who am not a subject of the Law made (C3)
myself a subject of the Law to those who are (C3)
the subjects of the Law, to win those who are
21 subject to the Law. ·To those who have no
Law, I was free of the Law myself (though not
free from God's law, being under the law of (C3)
22 Christ) to win those who have no Law. ·For (C3)
the weak I made myself weak. I made myself
all things to all men in order to save some at
23 any cost; ·and I still do this, for the sake of (C3)
the gospel, to have a share in its blessings. (C3)
24   All the runners at the stadium are trying to
win, but only one of them gets the prize. You
. must run in the same way, meaning to win. (C3)
(C4)
25 All the fighters at the games go into strict ·
training; they do this just to win a wreath
that will wither away, but we do it for a wreath
26 that will never wither. ·That is how I run, in- (C3)
tent on winning; that is how I fight, not beating (C4)
27 the air. ·I treat my body hard and make it
obey me, for, having been an announcer
myself, I should not want to be disqualified.

70

Week 1 Day 4
Four C's Meditations
on 1 Corinthians 8:1-9:27

1. Most Sacred Heart of Jesus, at first sight it seems that today's Scripture reading dealing with food offered to idols has no bearing on modern life in the West. Yet further reflection shows there is an underlying truth in Paul's teaching applicable to contemporary western man.

2. In essence, Paul teaches us that some acts, not immoral in themselves, could cause scandal if they are performed under certain circumstances.

3. Sometimes, however, these acts may actually be necessary, even if scandal is practically a certainty. Thus a priest, for example, might feel compelled to enter a house of ill-fame to rescue a woman who is threatening suicide. There are other times, however, when such necessity does not exist, and it would therefore be both unwise and imprudent to perform acts such as this.

This is what St. Paul had in mind when he cautioned his fellow Christians not to eat food sacrificed on pagan altars.

4.   He pointed out that people well-versed in Christian doctrine would know it was not immoral to eat food used in pagan sacrifices. But he also noted there were those who did not realize this truth, believing it would be sinful to eat such 'food. Consequently, if a knowledgeable Christian ate food of this sort in front of people improperly informed in the matter, he might well tempt them to eat some too. But if they were to do so, they would in fact be defiling their consciences, since they believed it to be a sinful act. *(For a discussion on the duty of obeying one's conscience even when falsely informed, see "The Catholic Catechism," p. 292)*

5.   Moreover, if they were non-Christians, they might also conclude that Christianity was a false religion since it tolerated a practice they considered immoral. Perhaps in our own time, Lord, it is the genuinely immoral conduct of Christians, who know what they do is against the teaching of Your Church, that does more damage to others than does the type of conduct just noted above.

6.   But even if this is true, it is still possible, today, to do what is not wrong in itself yet tempt others to sin. If we knowingly do so, and do so unnecessarily, we are sinning against charity and reveal the lack of pure consciences. For instance, if a married priest

of one of the Eastern Churches were to kiss his wife or hold hands with her in front of those who might think that all priests are bound to the law of celibacy, it might well tempt them to commit various types of sin. Or, if a "knowledgeable" person were to smoke or drink alcoholic beverages in the presence of those who believed such conduct was wrong, it might tempt them to do so also and thus violate their consciences.

7. Of course, Lord, proper education would help many to overcome their mistaken notions about certain types of lawful actions, but until such people are convinced to the contrary, it would be better for us to respect their consciences and not lead them into temptation. Obviously, we have reference only to those actions that are not necessary for us to perform in the conduct of our Christian lives.

8. Most Sacred Heart of Jesus, help us to be sensitive to the conscientiously-held convictions of others. We know also that if we are so disposed You will reward us in this life and in the next.

9. In chapter ten, Jesus, St. Paul notes the fact that he spent a good share of his ministry without receiving monetary support from those whom he served. He did this out of charity so as not to be a burden to them. May his example inspire others to work for the Church without pay. May they be filled with a spirit of self-sacrifice and joyfully contribute to the building up of Your Kingdom.

10. Most Merciful Savior, we next came across St. Paul's memorable words, "I made myself all things to all men in order to save some at any cost; and I still do this, for the sake of the gospel, to have a share in its blessings."[22] Some have concluded from this saying that Paul was a hypocrite. Not at all. He became all things to all men out of his deeply-rooted desire to share with them Your friendship, happiness and peace.

11. In order to fulfill his apostolic commission, St. Paul adapted himself to both the Jewish and Gentile worlds. Being a Jew, himself, he behaved as a Jew among the Jews so as not to scandalize them needlessly. Among the Gentiles, he behaved as a Gentile. He was free to do so since, as a Christian, he was no longer bound to Jewish ways which might offend Gentiles, or at least present unnecessary barriers between them and the acceptance of the Gospel.

12. In neither adaptation did St. Paul sin. And we must remember that the ultimate

74

purpose of his conduct was the salvation of souls.

13. Today, Lord, St. Paul's principle of adapting to the ways of different cultures, with the exception of sin, is just as valid as it was in the first century. If we wanted to gain converts among the Chinese, for example, and didn't know their language or their ways, or worse yet, knowing them refused to use them or adapt to them, we would not make much progress. Or if we sought to make converts among professional football players and refused to talk about football or compare Christianity with sports, we might make very little headway.

14. Lord, inspire us to be imaginative as well as charitable in our efforts to bring people into Your Church. With St. Paul, may we learn to become all things to all men while we live and promote our faith in You.

15. In the last portion of our meditation, Jesus, St. Paul, in fact, uses an analogy with sports.[23] He did so because the Corinthian Christians were familiar with the sports games that took place in various parts of the Roman Empire.

16. In his analogy, he stresses the necessity of a Christian living his life in such a way that it is geared toward winning an imperishable prize, the wreath of eternal life. He implies that constancy is of the utmost importance; constancy in confidence, constancy in maintaining a pure conscience, and constancy in

performing acts of seed-charity, since it is these that lead to a final victory over sin and death. Lord, may the imperishable crown of eternal life constantly be our goal. Amen.

The more you re-read these Scriptures and meditations, the more you will get out of them.

Please read and meditate on Chapter II and Chapter III, Paragraphs 1 to 9 in our "Prayers and Recommended Practices" book.

WEEK 1 DAY 5
1 Corinthians 10:1-11:34

A warning, and the lessons of Israel's history

1 **10** I want to remind you, brothers, how our fathers were all guided by a cloud above them and how they all passed through 2 the sea. •They were all baptized into Moses 3 in this cloud and in this sea; •all ate the same 4 spiritual food •and all drank the same spiritual drink, since they all drank from the spiritual rock that followed them as they went, and 5 that rock was Christ. •In spite of this, most of them failed to please God and their (C2) corpses littered the desert.

76

6 These things all happened as warnings[a] for us, not to have the wicked lusts for forbidden (C2)
7 things that they had. •Do not become idolaters as some of them did, for scripture says: (C2) *After sitting down to eat and drink, the people*
8 *got up to amuse themselves.[b]* •We must never (C2) fall into sexual immorality: some of them did, and twenty-three thousand met their downfall (C2)
9 in one day. •We are not to put the Lord to the test: some of them did, and they were
10 killed by snakes. •You must never complain: some of them did, and they were killed by the (C2) Destroyer.
11 All this happened to them as a warning, and it was written down to be a lesson for us
12 who are living at the end of the age. •The man (C2) who thinks he is safe must be careful that he
13 does not fall. •The trials that you have had to bear are no more than people normally (C1) have. You can trust God not to let you be tried beyond your strength, and with any trial he will give you a way out of it and the strength to bear it.

Sacrificial feasts. No compromise with idolatry

14 This is the reason, my dear brothers, why
15 you must keep clear of idolatry. •I say to you (C2) as sensible people: judge for yourselves what
16 I am saying. •The blessing-cup that we bless is a communion with the blood of Christ, and

the bread that we break is a communion with
17 the body of Christ. •The fact that there is only
one loaf means that, though there are many
of us, we form a single body because we all
18 have a share in this one loaf. •Look at the
other Israel, the race, where those who eat
the sacrifices are in communion with the al-
19 tar. •Does this mean that the food sacrificed
to idols has a real value, or that the idol itself
20 is real? •Not at all. It simply means that the
  sacrifices that they offer *they sacrifice to de-* (C2)
mons who are not God.[c] I have no desire to (C2)
21 see you in communion with demons. •You
cannot drink the cup of the Lord and the cup
of demons. You cannot take your share at the
table of the Lord and at the table of demons. (C2)
22 Do we want to make the Lord angry; are we
stronger than he is?

Food sacrificed to idols. Practical solutions

23   "For me there are no forbidden things,"
but not everything does good. True, there are
no forbidden things, but it is not everything
24 that helps the building to grow. •Nobody (C2)
should be looking for his own advantage, but
25 everybody for the other man's. •Do not hesi- (C 3)
tate to eat anything that is sold in butchers'
shops: there is no need to raise questions of
26 conscience; •for *the earth and everything that*
27 *is in it belong to the Lord.*[d] •If an unbeliever
invites you to his house, go if you want to,
and eat whatever is put in front of you, without asking questions just to satisfy con-
28 science. •But if someone says to you, "This
food was offered in sacrifice," then, out of
consideration for the man that told you, you (C 3)
should not eat it, for the sake of his scruples;

29 his scruples, you see, not your own. Why
should my freedom depend on somebody
30 else's conscience? •If I take my share with
thankfulness, why should I be blamed for
food for which I have thanked God?

31 Whatever you eat, whatever you drink, whatever you do at all, do it for the glory of (C3)
32 God. •Never do anything offensive to any- (C2) one—to Jews or Greeks or to the Church of
33 God; •just as I try to be helpful to everyone (C3) at all times, not anxious for my own advantage but for the advantage of everybody else, so that they may be saved.

1 **11** Take me for your model, as I take (C3) Christ.

C. DECORUM IN PUBLIC WORSHIP

Women's behavior at services

2 You have done well in remembering me so constantly and in maintaining the tradi- (C4)
3 tions just as I passed them on to you. •How- (C3) ever, what I want you to understand is that Christ is the head of every man, man is the head of woman, and God is the head of
4 Christ. •For a man to pray or prophesy with his head covered is a sign of disrespect to his
5 head.[a] •For a woman, however, it is a sign of (C3) disrespect to her head[b] if she prays or prophesies unveiled; she might as well have
6 her hair shaved off. •In fact, a woman who will not wear a veil ought to have her hair cut (C2) off. If a woman is ashamed to have her hair cut off or shaved, she ought to wear a veil.
7 A man should certainly not cover his head, (C2) since he is the image of God and reflects God's glory; but woman is the reflection of
8 man's glory. •For man did not come from
9 woman; no, woman came from man; •and man was not created for the sake of woman, but woman was created for the sake of man.
10 That is the argument for women's covering their heads with a symbol of the authority over them, out of respect for the angels.[c]
11 However, though woman cannot do without

79

man, neither can man do without woman, in
12 the Lord; •woman may come from man, but
man is born of woman—both come from
God.

13 Ask yourselves if it is fitting for a woman
14 to pray to God without a veil; •and whether
nature itself does not tell you that long hair
15 on a man is nothing to be admired, •while a
woman, who was given her hair as a covering,
thinks long hair her glory?

16 To anyone who might still want to argue:
it is not the custom with us, nor in the
churches of God.

The Lord's Supper

17 Now that I am on the subject of instruc- (C2)
tions, I cannot say that you have done well
in holding meetings that do you more harm
18 than good. •In the first place, I hear that when
you all come together as a community, there
are separate factions among you, and I half (C2)
19 believe it—•since there must no doubt be
separate groups among you, to distinguish
20 those who are to be trusted. •The point is,
when you hold these meetings, it is not the

21 Lord's Supper*d* that you are eating, •since when the time comes to eat, everyone is in such a hurry to start his own supper that one person goes hungry while another is getting (C2)

22 drunk. •Surely you have homes for eating and drinking in? Surely you have enough respect (C3) for the community of God not to make poor people embarrassed? What am I to say to you? Congratulate you? I cannot congratulate you on this.

23 For this is what I received from the Lord, and in turn passed on to you: that on the same night that he was betrayed, the Lord Jesus

24 took some bread, •and thanked God for it and broke it, and he said, "This is my body, which

25 is for you; do this as a memorial of me." •In the same way he took the cup after supper, and said, "This cup is the new covenant in my blood. Whenever you drink it, do this as

26 a memorial of me." •Until the Lord comes, therefore, every time you eat this bread and drink this cup, you are proclaiming his death,

27 and so anyone who eats the bread or drinks without recognizing the Body is eating and drinking unworthily towards the body and (C2) blood of the Lord.

28 Everyone is to recollect himself before (C3)
29 eating this bread and drinking this cup; •because a person who eats and drinks without (C2) recognizing the Body is eating and drinking

30 his own condemnation. •In fact that is why many of you are weak and ill and some of you

31 have died. •If only we recollected ourselves,
32 we should not be punished like that. •But when the Lord does punish us like that, it is to correct us and stop us from being condemned with the world.

33 So to sum up, my dear brothers, when you meet for the Meal, wait for one another.

34 Anyone who is hungry should eat at home, and then your meeting will not bring your condemnation. The other matters I shall adjust when I come.

Week 1 Day 5
Four C's Meditations
on 1 Corinthians 10:1-11:34

1. In today's reading, Lord, St. Paul reminded the Corinthian Christians of the blessings You showered upon the Israelites as they journeyed from Egypt to Canaan centuries earlier.[24] Nonetheless, most of the Israelites turned against You by committing a variety of sins, and many were punished by death. St. Paul's reference to the Israelites' sins, especially the sin of sexual immorality, and his words on divine punishment served as a warning to the Corinthians as, indeed, they do for us today.

2. Sexual perversion is so widespread in our culture that even some "Catholic" moral theologians, deviating from the unchangeable teachings of Your Catholic Church, hold that many immoral sexual practices are either

moral or they are not very serious. *(For a discussion on the seriousness of sexual perversion, see "The Catholic Catechism," p. 120; and for a summary of the Church's teaching on sexual pleasure see pages 352-356.)*

3. Lord, may we always turn to You and Your Blessed Mother for protection against the ever-present temptations against sexual purity. Also guide parents as they discuss the delicate topic of human sexuality with their children. Help them to realize that it is primarily upon them that this charitable duty falls. Help them to be neither too severe nor too lenient in the handling of the subject. Above all, Most Merciful Savior, help them to give their children good practical advice on how to maintain chastity or self-control in matters of sex.

4. Most Sacred Heart of Jesus, in today's Scripture reading St. Paul also warns us against the sin of presumption: "The man who thinks he is safe must be careful that he

does not fall."[25] We must not presume we will never sin again or never commit a particular sin. To think this way is foolish and can only slacken our trust in You as the ultimate Source and sustainer of our virtues.

5.   In fact, presumption is a type of pride or self-centeredness. As such, it opposes the virtue of seed-charity. St. Paul's warning of presumption reminds us of the saying in the Book of Proverbs that "Pride goes before destruction, a haughty spirit before a fall."[26] As a rule of thumb, Lord, we might say that when we are smugly satisfied with our spiritual and moral progress, we had better examine our consciences very carefully in the light of the Church's teaching and pray to You for enlightenment.

6.   Next, Lord, St. Paul warns the Christians that it is incompatible to participate in both pagan sacrifices and in the Eucharist.[27] To sacrifice to the false gods of paganism, says St. Paul, is to sacrifice to demons who inspire Christians to abandon the worship of God alone. Jesus, to pay homage to false gods of any sort would be to place them on at least an equal footing with Yourself. In effect, it would be a denial of Your rightful primacy over the universe.

7.   To place created things on an equal or superior level to You, Lord is a form of idolatry, whether they are demons or the false gods of money, sex, power, alcohol, drugs, or even our loved ones. Most Sacred Heart of Jesus, we can never tire asking You for the

gift of seed-charity so we can love You as we ought. And when we do love You properly, we see the whole world of creation in its true God-centered perspective. Consequently, we see far more clearly the relative value of everything else. And we love You, Lord, in our family members, in our friends, in our associates and in our neighbors, as well as through prayer and worship.

8. Lord, at the beginning of chapter eleven, St. Paul says most strikingly that the Corinthian Christians are to follow him as their model — even as he took You for his model. At first glance, this command might seem to reflect the worst type of conceit. But it really does not.

9. Why not, someone might ask? Because, St. Paul was the Corinthians' spiritual father who kept Your teaching pure and undefiled. Furthermore, he knew that through Your grace he had acquired many virtues. He also knew that when he sinned, he had repented and confessed his sinfulness thus gaining Your favor. There was, then, in St. Paul the element of simple honesty, rather than conceit. And his thoughts, words and actions were indeed worthy of imitation.

10. Next, Jesus, St. Paul made a few remarks about the proper headdress for men and women when they pray. [28] He is theologically correct about the great responsibility You have given men for the welfare of women. [29] But when he says men must pray with their heads uncovered and

85

women with their heads covered as a reflection of this theological teaching, he refers only to custom, not to the universal moral or natural law. Nonetheless, this passage serves to show us that the Church can rightly expect the faithful to observe certain disciplines, such as mandatory priestly celibacy and a special measure of spiritual discipline on Fridays, even though they are not revealed by You. Nor are they an essential part of the moral law. However, they do promote good order and the practice of seed-charity.

11. Lastly, St. Paul wrote of the importance of being properly prepared for Mass, [30] and he chastised those who attended Mass intoxicated and in an irreverent manner. He stressed the importance of entering into a celebration reverently and being conscious of the fact that You are really present under the outward forms of bread and wine. A presence which he referred to as Your Body and Blood. And our Faith tells us that this is the same Body and Blood which You offered to the Father on Calvary for our salvation.

12. Lord, may we always properly prepare ourselves for the Holy Sacrifice of the Mass by examining our consciences, confessing our sins, and reflecting on what it is we are about to celebrate and receive from the hands of Your priest. The Mass is the Church's greatest act of adoration of You. May we always participate in its actions with deep faith and seed-charity. Amen.

Try to experience the gift of God's peace by slowly re-reading and re-meditating on the Scripture for today, and asking the Holy Spirit for this gift which the world cannot give.

Please read and meditate on Chapter III, Paragraphs 10 to 29 in our "Prayers and Recommended Practices" book.

WEEK 1 DAY 6
1 Corinthians 12:1-13:13

Spiritual gifts

1 **12**Now my dear brothers, I want to clear up a wrong impression about spiritual
2 gifts. •You remember that, when you were pagans, whenever you felt irresistibly drawn,
3 it was toward dumb idols? •It is for that rea-

son that I want you to understand that on the one hand no one can be speaking under the influence of the Holy Spirit and say, "Curse (C2) Jesus," and on the other hand, no one can say, "Jesus is Lord," unless he is under the (C1) influence of the Holy Spirit.

The variety and the unity of gifts

4 There is a variety of gifts but always the 5 same Spirit; ·there are all sorts of service to 6 be done, but always to the same Lord; ·working in all sorts of different ways in different people, it is the same God who is working 7 in all of them. ·The particular way in which the Spirit is given to each person is for a good 8 purpose. ·One may have the gift of preaching with wisdom given him by the Spirit; another may have the gift of preaching instruction 9 given him by the same Spirit; ·and another the gift of faith given by the same Spirit; another again the gift of healing, through this one 10 Spirit; ·one, the power of miracles; another, prophecy; another the gift of recognizing spirits; another the gift of tongues and an-11 other the ability to interpret them. ·All these are the work of one and the same Spirit, who distributes different gifts to different people just as he chooses.

The analogy of the body

12 Just as a human body, though it is made up of many parts, is a single unit because all these parts, though many, make one body, so 13 it is with Christ. ·In the one Spirit we were all baptized, Jews as well as Greeks, slaves as well as citizens, and one Spirit was given to us all to drink.

14 Nor is the body to be identified with any 15 one of its many parts. ·If the foot were to say, "I am not a hand and so I do not belong to the body," would that mean that it stopped 16 being part of the body? ·If the ear were to say,

"I am not an eye, and so I do not belong to the body," would that mean that it was not 17 a part of the body? •If your whole body was just one eye, how would you hear anything? If it was just one ear, how would you smell anything?

18 Instead of that, God put all the sepa- 19 rate parts into the body on purpose. •If all the parts were the same, how could it 20 be a body? •As it is, the parts are many but 21 the body is one. •The eye cannot say to the hand, "I do not need you," nor can the head say to the feet, "I do not need you."

22 What is more, it is precisely the parts of the body that seem to be the weakest which 23 are the indispensable ones; •and it is the least honorable parts of the body that we clothe with the greatest care. So our more improper 24 parts get decorated •in a way that our more proper parts do not need. God has arranged the body so that more dignity is given to the 25 parts which are without it, •and so that there may not be disagreements inside the body, (C2) but that each part may be equally concerned (C3) 26 for all the others. •If one part is hurt, all parts are hurt with it. If one part is given special honor, all parts enjoy it.

27 Now you together are Christ's body; but

28 each of you is a different part of it. •In the Church, God has given the first place to apostles, the second to prophets, the third to teachers; after them, miracles, and after them the gift of healing; helpers, good leaders,
29 those with many languages. •Are all of them apostles, or all of them prophets, or all of them teachers? Do they all have the gift of
30 miracles, •or all have the gift of healing? Do all speak strange languages, and all interpret them?

The order of importance in spiritual gifts. Love

31 Be ambitious for the higher gifts. And I am (C4) going to show you a way that is better than any of them.

1 **13** If I have all the eloquence of men or of angels, but speak without love, I am (C2) simply a gong booming or a cymbal clashing.
2 If I have the gift of prophecy, understanding all the mysteries there are, and knowing everything, and if I have faith in all its fullness, (C1) to move mountains, but without love, then I (C2)
3 am nothing at all. •If I give away all that I possess, piece by piece, and if I even let them take my body to burn it, but am without love, (C2) it will do me no good whatever.
4 Love is always patient and kind; it is (C3) never jealous; love is never boastful or con- (C2)
5 ceited; •it is never rude or selfish; it does
6 not take offense, and is not resentful. •Love takes no pleasure in other people's sins but (C3)
7 delights in the truth; •it is always ready to (C3) excuse, to trust, to hope, and to endure what- (C4) ever comes.
8 Love does not come to an end. But if there (C3) are gifts of prophecy, the time will come when they must fail; or the gift of languages, it will not continue for ever; and knowledge—for this, too, the time will come when
9 it must fail. •For our knowledge is imperfect
10 and our prophesying is imperfect; •but once perfection comes, all imperfect things will

11 disappear. ·When I was a child, I used to talk like a child, and think like a child, and argue like a child, but now I am a man, all childish
12 ways are put behind me. ·Now we are seeing a dim reflection in a mirror; but then we shall be seeing face to face. The knowledge that I have now is imperfect; but then I shall know as fully as I am known. (C1)
13 In short, there are three things that last: faith, hope and love; and the greatest of these is love. (C3)

Week 1 Day 6
Four C's Meditations
on 1 Corinthians 12:1-13:13

1. Jesus, Savior, in today's meditation we came across some of St. Paul's most memorable writing. In it he mentioned various special gifts You provide for Your Church through God the Holy Spirit. He also compared Your Church to the human body. Finally, he underscored the importance of the virtue of charity. *(The Church commonly refers to the special gifts mentioned in chapter twelve as charisms, that is, gifts of grace given to some for the good of others.*

These are to be contrasted with other supernatural gifts such as the theological virtues of faith, hope and seed-charity which are intended for all Christians.)

2.   By the way of prelude, St. Paul noted that we can only call You Lord (with conviction), i.e. God, under the influence of the Holy Spirit. What marvelous evidence this is, then, of the Holy Spirit's presence within us! *(We can, however, possess the gift of faith, but lack seed-charity, thereby jeopardizing our salvation.)*

3.   The Spirit gives individual Christians special gifts of grace, or charisms, according to the Church's needs.[31] Some may have one or more types of charisms, others may have other kinds. All of the recipients, however, are expected to use their charisms for the well-being of the entire body of the Church. Lord, whatever charisms we possess, help us always realize that they are given to us, not primarily for our own welfare, but for that of the Church. Also, Lord, help us not to be hesitant in using them. And may we use them generously, remembering that one day we will have to render an accounting for them before Your judgment seat.[32]

4.   Most Sacred Heart of Jesus, St. Paul's words help us realize how important each Christian is for the building up of Your Mystical Body, the Church. Each of us, as a part of Your providential plan, is like a vital organ of the human body. And if we do not contribute to the Church's spiritual growth and strength, the whole Mystical Body suffers in one way or another.

5. How rarely many of us think of this. Actually, a deliberate failure to exercise a charism would be a form of selfishness. By withholding our assistance we also hurt ourselves, since we are failing to receive an increase of sanctifying grace. Moreover, we do not experience the true happiness, inner peace and joy which result from the charitable exercise of our spiritual gifts. Nor should we forget, Most Merciful Lord, that the charitable exercise of these gifts furthers the work of reparation, or satisfaction, for the countless offenses committed against Your Sacred Heart. *(For more information on reparation, see "The Catholic Catechism," pp. 431-432.)*

6. Nor, Jesus, should we be distressed if we notice that some people have more or greater charisms than we do. This is due to Your mysterious, unfathomable plan for the Church and mankind. And the fact that one person has more or greater charisms than another does not necessarily tell us anything about the sanctity of that person.

7. There are canonized saints, for instance who apparently possessed no extraordinary spiritual gifts such as prophecy or the working of miracles. But what gifts they did have, they exercised exceptionally well and with a generous love. On the other side of the coin, we should also remember the horrendous fate of satan, the most gifted and intelligent of all of Your creatures.

8. Next, Most Merciful Savior, in chapter 13, St. Paul wrote about seed-charity, the

greatest of the infused virtues. We have seen seed-charity mentioned over and over again in the course of our Four C's meditations, but nowhere is it described better than in this chapter. *(For more on charity and the other theological virtues, see "The Catholic Catechism," pp. 194-197.)*

9. The Greek word used by St. Paul for seed-charity is *agape*, and is translated as "love" in the "Jerusalem Bible." Unfortunately, no single English word can do the term *agape* justice. It is a love which is selfless, unselfish, and self-sacrificing. Its primary object is You, Lord, and the Father and the Holy Spirit. It seeks to glorify the Trinitarian God as the highest good which exists.

10. Secondarily, *agape* is meant to be directed towards our fellow humans, both friends and foes. It seeks, especially, their salvation and sanctification.

11.   It was in the spirit of selfless love *(agape)*, Lord, that You became one of us and sacrificed Yourself for us on the Cross. And it is in the spirit of selfless love *(agape)* that You will continue to help us, if we turn to You in trust and reciprocate with the selfless love *(agape)* You constantly give Your friends.

12.   Jesus, St. Paul tells us essentially that we may have any number of spiritual gifts, including faith and hope, but if we do not have *agape*, i.e., seed-charity, (and he implies that it must be used), we are not in the state of grace, we do not enjoy Your friendship and we cannot enter into the Kingdom of Heaven. It follows, then, that Christians may obtain *agape*, assuming they do not already have it, through a sincere repentance of their sins and the reception of the sacrament of Penance. Jesus, thank You from the bottom of our hearts for meriting the priceless gift of *agape* for us on the Cross. Amen.

Try to read these Scripture passages and meditations several times a day in a reflective manner. Each time you do so, the Holy Spirit will give you more insights.

Please read and meditate on Chapter III, Paragraphs 30 to 41 in our "Prayers and Recommended Practices" book.

WEEK 1 DAY 7
1 Corinthians 14:1-16:24

**Spiritual gifts: their respective importance
in the community**

1 **14** You must want love more than any- (C3)
thing else; but still hope for the spiritual
2 gifts as well, especially prophecy. •Anybody (C1)
with the gift of tongues speaks to God, but
not to other people; because nobody understands him when he talks in the spirit about
3 mysterious things. •On the other hand, the
man who prophesies does talk to other people, to their improvement, their encourage- (C3)
4 ment and their consolation. •The one with the
gift of tongues talks for his own benefit, but (C3)
the man who prophesies does so for the bene-
5 fit of the community. •While I should like you

all to have the gift of tongues, I would much
rather you could prophesy, since the man
who prophesies is of greater importance than
the man with the gift of tongues, unless of
course the latter offers an interpretation so (C3)
that the church may get some benefit.

6   Now suppose, my dear brothers, I am

someone with the gift of tongues, and I come to visit you, what use shall I be if all my talking reveals nothing new, tells you nothing, and neither inspires you nor instructs 7 you? ·Think of a musical instrument, a flute or a harp: if one note on it cannot be distinguished from another, how can you tell what 8 tune is being played? ·Or if no one can be sure which call the trumpet has sounded, who 9 will be ready for the attack? ·It is the same with you: if your tongue does not produce intelligible speech, how can anyone know what you are saying? You will be talking to 10 the air. ·There are any number of different languages in the world, and not one of them 11 is meaningless, ·but if I am ignorant of what the sounds mean, I am a savage to the man who is speaking, and he is a savage 12 to me. ·It is the same in your own case: since (C3) you aspire to spiritual gifts, concentrate on those which will grow to benefit the community.

13 That is why anybody who has the gift of tongues must pray for the power of interpret-14 ing them. ·For if I use this gift in my prayers, my spirit may be praying but my mind is left 15 barren. ·What is the answer to that? Surely I should pray not only with the spirit but with the mind as well? And sing praises not only 16 with the spirit but with the mind as well?·Any uninitiated person will never be able to say Amen to your thanksgiving, if you only bless God with the spirit, for he will have no idea 17 what you are saying. ·However well you make your thanksgiving, the other gets no 18 benefit from it. ·I thank God that I have a 19 greater gift of tongues than all of you, ·but when I am in the presence of the community I would rather say five words that mean something than ten thousand words in a tongue.

20 Brothers, you are not to be childish in your (C2) outlook. You can be babies as far as wicked-

ness is concerned, but mentally you must be ^(C3) 21 adult. •In the written Law it says: *Through men speaking strange languages and through the lips of foreigners, I shall talk to the nation, and still they will not listen to me, says* 22 *the Lord.ª* •You see then, that the strange languages are meant to be a sign not for believers but for unbelievers, while on the other hand, prophecy is a sign not for unbelievers 23 but for believers. •So that any uninitiated people or unbelievers, coming into a meeting of the whole church where everybody was speaking in tongues, would say you were all 24 mad; •but if you were all prophesying and an unbeliever or uninitiated person came in, he would find himself analyzed and judged by 25 everyone speaking; •he would find his secret thoughts laid bare, and then fall on his face and worship God, declaring that *God is among you indeed.ᵇ*

Regulating spiritual gifts

26 So, my dear brothers, what conclusion is to be drawn? At all your meetings, let everyone be ready with a psalm or a sermon or a revelation, or ready to use his gift of tongues ^(C3) or to give an interpretation; but it must always

98

27 be for the common good. •If there are people present with the gift of tongues, let only two or three, at the most, be allowed to use it, and only one at a time, and there must be some-
28 one to interpret. •If there is no interpreter present, they must keep quiet in church and
29 speak only to themselves and to God. •As for prophets, let two or three of them speak, and
30 the others attend to them. •If one of the listeners receives a revelation, then the man
31 who is already speaking should stop. •For you can all prophesy in turn, so that everybody will learn something and everybody will
32 be encouraged. •Prophets can always control
33 their prophetic spirits, •since God is not a God of disorder but of peace.

As in all the churches of the saints,
34 women are to remain quiet at meetings since they have no permission to speak; they must keep in the background as the Law itself lays
35 it down. •If they have any questions to ask, they should ask their husbands at home: it does not seem right for a woman to raise her voice at meetings.

36 Do you think the word of God came out of yourselves? Or that it has come only to
37 you? •Anyone who claims to be a prophet or inspired ought to recognize that what I am writing to you is a command from the Lord.

38 Unless he recognizes this, you should not recognize him.

39 And so, my dear brothers, by all means be (C3) ambitious to prophesy, do not suppress the

40 gift of tongues, ·but let everything be done (C2) with propriety and in order.

III. THE RESURRECTION OF THE DEAD

The fact of the resurrection

1 **15** Brothers, I want to remind you of the (C3) gospel I preached to you, the gospel (C3) that you received and in which you are firmly (C4)

2 established; ·because the gospel will save you (C1) only if you keep believing exactly what I preached to you—believing anything else (C2) will not lead to anything.

3 Well then, in the first place, I taught you (C3) what I had been taught myself, namely that Christ died for our sins, in accordance with

4 the scriptures; ·that he was buried; and that he was raised to life on the third day, in ac-

5 cordance with the scriptures; ·that he ap- peared first to Cephas and secondly to the

6 Twelve. ·Next he appeared to more than five hundred of the brothers at the same time, most of whom are still alive, though some

7 have died; ·then he appeared to James, and

8 then to all the apostles; ·and last of all he appeared to me too; it was as though I was born when no one expected it.

9 I am the least of the apostles; in fact, since (C2) I persecuted the Church of God, I hardly

10 deserve the name apostle; ·but by God's grace that is what I am, and the grace that he gave me has not been fruitless. On the con- (C3) trary, I, or rather the grace of God that is with me, have worked harder than any of the (C4)

11 others; ·but what matters is that I preach what they preach, and this is what you all be- lieved.

100

12 Now if Christ raised from the dead is what has been preached, how can some of you be saying that there is no resurrection of the (C2) 13 dead? ·If there is no resurrection of the dead, 14 Christ himself cannot have been raised, ·and if Christ has not been raised then our preaching is useless and your believing it is useless; (C1) 15 indeed, we are shown up as witnesses who (C2) have committed perjury before God, because · we swore in evidence before God that he had 16 raised Christ to life. ·For if the dead are not 17 raised, Christ has not been raised, ·and if (C2) Christ has not been raised, you are still in 18 your sins. ·And what is more serious, all who 19 have died in Christ have perished. ·If our (C1) hope in Christ has been for this life only, we are the most unfortunate of all people.

20 But Christ has in fact been raised from the dead, the first-fruits of all who have fallen 21 asleep. ·Death came through one man and in the same way the resurrection of the dead has 22 come through one man.. ·Just as all men die in Adam, so all men will be brought to life 23 in Christ; ·but all of them in their proper order: Christ as the first-fruits and then, after the coming of Christ, those who belong to 24 him. ·After that will come the end, when he hands over the kingdom to God the Father, having done away with every sovereignty, au-

25 thority and power. ·For he must be king *until*
26 *he has put all his enemies under his feet*[a] ·and
the last of the enemies to be destroyed is
death, for everything is to be *put under his*
27 *feet.* ·—Though when it is said that *everything*
is subjected, this clearly cannot include the
28 One who subjected everything to him. ·And
when everything is subjected to him, then the
Son himself will be subject in his turn to the
One who subjected all things to him, so that
God may be all in all.

29   If this were not true, what do people hope
to gain by being baptized for the dead? If the
dead are not ever going to be raised, why be
30 baptized on their behalf? ·What about our-   (C3)
selves? Why are we living under a constant
31 threat? ·I face death every day, brothers, and   (C4)
I can swear it by the pride that I take in you
32 in Christ Jesus our Lord. ·If my motives were   (C2)
only human ones, what good would it do me
33 to fight the wild animals at Ephesus? ·You   (C3)
say: *Let us eat and drink today; tomorrow we*   (C2)
shall be dead.[b] You must stop being led
astray: "Bad friends ruin the noblest peo-
34 ple."[c] ·Come to your senses, behave prop-   (C3)
erly, and leave sin alone; there are some of   (C2)
you who seem not to know God at all; you
should be ashamed.   (C2)

The manner of the resurrection

35   Someone may ask, "How are dead people
raised, and what sort of body do they have
36 when they come back?" ·They are stupid
questions. Whatever you sow in the ground
37 has to die before it is given new life ·and the
thing that you sow is not what is going to
come; you sow a bare grain, say of wheat or
38 something like that, ·and then God gives it
the sort of body that he has chosen: each sort
of seed gets its own sort of body.

39   Everything that is flesh is not the same
flesh: there is human flesh, animals' flesh, the
40 flesh of birds and the flesh of fish. ·Then there

are heavenly bodies and there are earthly
bodies; but the heavenly bodies have a beauty
of their own and the earthly bodies a different
41 one. ·The sun has its brightness, the moon
a different brightness, and the stars a different
brightness, and the stars differ from each
42 other in brightness. ·It is the same with the
resurrection of the dead: the thing that is
sown is perishable but what is raised is imper-
43 ishable; ·the thing that is sown is contemptible but what is raised is glorious; the thing
that is sown is weak but what is raised is
44 powerful; ·when it is sown it embodies the
soul, when it is raised it embodies the spirit.

If the soul has its own embodiment, so
does the spirit have its own embodiment.
45 The first *man,* Adam, as scripture says, *became a living soul;* but the last Adam has
46 become a life-giving spirit. ·That is, first the
one with the soul, not the spirit, and after
47 that, the one with the spirit. ·The first man,
being from the earth, is earthly by nature; the
48 second man is from heaven. ·As this earthly
man was, so are we on earth; and as the heav-
49 enly man is, so are we in heaven. ·And we,
who have been modeled on the earthly man,
will be modeled on the heavenly man.

50   Or else, brothers, put it this way: flesh and
blood cannot inherit the kingdom of God:
and the perishable cannot inherit what lasts
51 for ever. ·I will tell you something that has
been secret: that we are not all going to die,
52 but we shall all be changed. ·This will be
instantaneous, in the twinkling of an eye,
when the last trumpet sounds. It will sound,
and the dead will be raised, imperishable, and
53 we shall be changed as well, ·because our
present perishable nature must put on
imperishability and this mortal nature must
put on immortality.

A hymn of triumph. Conclusion

54   When this perishable nature has put on

imperishability, and when this mortal nature
has put on immortality, then the words of
scripture will come true: *Death is swallowed*
55 *up in victory.* •*Death, where is your* victory?
56 *Death, where is your sting?*ᵈ •Now the sting (C2)
of death is sin, and sin gets its power from
57 the Law. •So let us thank God for giving us
the victory through our Lord Jesus Christ.

58   Never give in then, my dear brothers. (C3)
never admit defeat; keep on working at the (C4)
Lord's work always, knowing that, in the
Lord, you cannot be laboring in vain.

CONCLUSION

Commendations. Greetings

1 **16**Now about the collection made for the
saints: you are to do as I told the
2 churches in Galatia to do. •Every Sunday, (C4)
each one of you must put aside what he can
afford, so that collections need not be made (C3)
3 after I have come. •When I am with you, I
will send your offering to Jerusalem by the (C3)
hand of whatever men you give letters of
4 reference to; •if it seems worth while for me
to go too, they can travel with me.
5   I shall be coming to you after I have passed

through Macedonia—and I am doing no
6 more than pass through Macedonia—·and I
may be staying with you, perhaps even passing the winter, to make sure that it is you who
send me on my way wherever my travels take
7 me. ·As you see, I do not want to make it only
a passing visit to you and I hope to spend
some time with you, the Lord permitting.
8 In any case I shall be staying at Ephesus until
9 Pentecost ·because a big and important door
has opened for my work and there is a great
deal of opposition.   (C2)

10   If Timothy comes, show him that he has
nothing to be afraid of in you: like me, he is   (C3)
11 doing the Lord's work, ·and nobody is to be   (C2)
scornful of him. Send him happily on his way   (C3)
to come back to me; the brothers and I are
12 waiting for him. ·As for our brother Apollos,
I begged him to come to you with the brothers but he was quite firm that he did not want
to go yet and he will come as soon as he can.   (C3)
13   Be awake to all the dangers; stay firm in   (C4)
14 the faith; be brave and be strong. ·Let every-   (C1)
thing you do be done in love.

15   There is something else to ask you, broth-   (C3)
ers. You know how the Stephanas family,
who were the first-fruits of Achaia, have   (C3)
16 really worked hard to help the saints. ·Well,   (C4)
I want you in your turn to put yourselves at   (C3)
the service of people like this, and anyone
17 who helps and works with them. ·I am de-
lighted that Stephanas, Fortunatus and
Achaicus have arrived; they make up for your
18 absence. ·They have settled my mind, and
yours too; I hope you appreciate men like
this.

19   All the churches of Asia send you greet-   (C3)
ings. Aquila and Prisca, with the church that
meets at their house, send you their warmest
20 wishes, in the Lord. ·All the brothers send
you their greetings. Greet one another with
a holy kiss.   (C3)
21   This greeting is in my own hand—Paul.

22 If anyone does not love the Lord, a curse (C2) on him. "Maran atha."*a*

23 The grace of the Lord Jesus be with you.

24 My love is with you all in Christ Jesus.

Week 1 Day 7
Four C's Meditations
on 1 Corinthians 14:1-16:24

1. Lord, in the first part of today's reading, St. Paul notes once more the superiority of seed-charity.[33] However, he is more intent here on emphasizing the excellence of the special supernatural gift of prophecy, which he describes as the ability to know and understand divine mysteries, i.e., the hidden things of God.[34]

2. In chapter 14, St. Paul contrasts prophecy with the special gift of tongues (glossalalia). Apparently, there were some in the Corinthian Church who were making too much of speaking in tongues, while tending to neglect prophecy.

3. Speaking in tongues, St. Paul maintained, is good in itself but it is not primarily meant for the good of others. Rather it is for the benefit of the individual recipient who addresses it only to God. *(This particular type of speaking in tongues seems to consist of ecstatic utterances inspired by the Holy Spirit, which no one without a special gift of interpretation is able to understand, not even the speaker himself. Its purpose is to praise God.)*

4. As you recall, Lord, St. Paul declared that he himself had the gift, but he downplayed its importance. "I thank God that I have a greater gift of tongues than all of you, but when I am in the presence of the community I would rather say five words that mean something than ten thousand words in a tongue."[35]

5. In praise of prophecy, on the other hand, St. Paul noted that the gift is meant to be directed "to other people, to their improvement, their encouragement and their consolation."[36] Used in this manner, prophecy would also be an exercise in seed-charity. Moreover, St. Paul encouraged the Corinthians to seek other charisms which would also benefit the community, charisms such as supernatural healing and the ability to preach with wisdom. Even the gift of tongues, Paul adds, could aid the community, if there were an interpretation accompanying its use.

6. O divine Savior of the world, grant us the particular charisms You want us to use for the improvement of our fellow Christians, and inspire us to use them with constant charity.

7. Jesus, Our Lord, in chapter 15, St. Paul speaks of Your bodily Resurrection from the dead. His words reflect a deep penetration into this great mystery.

8. He dwells on this dogma of the Church because there were those who, lacking the virtue of faith, denied it. In support of the Resurrection, Lord, St. Paul points out that Peter and the other Apostles and disciples witnessed it. Not only did they witness it, but most of them were still alive at the time of St. Paul's writing. Thus doubters and disbelievers could consult them if they wished.

9. Lord, today we accept this doctrine, in the first instance, because of the testimony of Your Apostles. In the course of their ministry, they proclaimed it repeatedly. And because of their proclamation, they often risked their physical safety, and even their lives, as the Acts of the Apostles attested. [37] Jesus, if You were not raised physically from the dead, why did the Apostles constantly risk danger to

declare it? They certainly gained no worldly prestige or power or wealth from doing so, and most of them were put to death for insisting on it. St. Paul himself said that if the doctrine of the Resurrection were not true:

10. "...then our preaching is useless and your believing it is useless; indeed, we are shown up as witnesses who have committed perjury before God, because we swore in evidence before God that he had raised Christ to life...and if Christ has not been raised, you are still in your sins. And what is more serious, all who have died in Christ have perished."[38]

11. Also, Lord, St. Paul notes that because of Your Resurrection we also shall be raised

109

bodily from the dead. He says our bodies at death are like perishable seeds sown in the ground. But, also, like sown seeds they will become transformed; transformed at the resurrection and brought forth as something new and imperishable.

12. Most Sacred Heart of Jesus, we look forward with hope to the time when we shall be raised bodily from the dead. May we die in the state of grace, so that wonderfully transformed and glorified in our resurrected bodies, we may enjoy You forever in the company of Your angels and saints. *(For more on the doctrine of the Resurrection, see "The Catholic Catechism," pp. 38, 145-146.)*

13. In the concluding chapter of our meditation, Lord, St. Paul urges the Corinthian Christians to be steadfast in the Faith and to perform various acts of charity for their fellow Christians, such as contributing to the needy of the Church in Jerusalem.[39]

14. May we also, Lord, persevere in the Faith, which has been maintained in its fullness in the Catholic Church. And may we, as Your representatives do everything with seed-charity. Amen.

Try to read these Scripture passages and meditations in a reflective manner every day. The Holy Spirit will reveal more insights to you each time you do so.

Please read and meditate on Chapter III, Paragraphs 42 to 60 of our "Prayers and Recommended Practices" book.

2 Corinthians

THE SECOND LETTER
OF PAUL TO THE
CHURCH AT CORINTH

INTRODUCTION

Address and greetings. Thanksgiving

1 **1** From Paul, appointed by God to be an
apostle of Christ Jesus, and from Timothy,
one of the brothers, to the church of God at
Corinth and to all the saints in the whole of
2 Achaia. ·Grace and peace to you from God
our Father and the Lord Jesus Christ.

3   Blessed be the God and Father of our Lord
Jesus Christ, a gentle Father and the God of
4 all consolation, ·who comforts us in all our   (C3)
sorrows, so that we can offer others, in their
sorrows, the consolation that we have re-
5 ceived from God ourselves. ·Indeed, as the
sufferings of Christ overflow to us, so,
through Christ, does our consolation over-

111

6 flow. •When we are made to suffer, it is for (C3)
your consolation and salvation. When, instead, we are comforted, this should be a
consolation to you, supporting you in pa-
tiently bearing the same sufferings as we (C3)
7 bear. •And our hope for you is confident, (C4)
since we know that, sharing our sufferings, (C1)
you will also share our consolations.

8 For we should like you to realize, brothers, (C3)
that the things we had to undergo in Asia
were more of a burden than we could carry,
so that we despaired of coming through alive.
9 Yes, we were carrying our own death warrant
with us, and it has taught us not to rely on
ourselves but only on God, who raises the (C1)
10 dead to life. •And he saved us from dying,
as he will save us again; yes, that is our firm (C1)
hope in him, that in the future he will save
11 us again. •You must all join in the prayers for
us: the more people there are asking for help (C3)
for us, the more will be giving thanks when
it is granted to us.

I. SOME RECENT EVENTS
REVIEWED

Why Paul changed his plans

12 There is one thing we are proud of, and
our conscience tells us it is true: that we have
always treated everybody, and especially (C3)
you, with the reverence and sincerity which
come from God, and by the grace of God
we have done this without ulterior motives.
13 There are no hidden meanings in our letters (C3)
besides what you can read for yourselves and
14 understand. •And I hope that, although you
do not know us very well yet, you will have
come to recognize, when the day of our Lord
Jesus comes, that you can be as proud of us
as we are of you.
15 Because I was so sure of this, I had meant
to come to you first, so that you would benefit

16 doubly; •staying with you before going to Macedonia and coming back to you again on the way back from Macedonia, for you to

17 see me on my way to Judaea. •Do you think I was not sure of my own intentions when I planned this? Do you really think that when I am making my plans, my motives are ordi (C2) nary human ones, and that I say Yes, yes,

18 and No, no, at the same time? •I swear by God's truth, there is no Yes and No about

19 what we say to you. •The Son of God, the (C3) Christ Jesus that we proclaimed among you— I mean Silvanus and Timothy and I—was (C2) never Yes and No: with him it was always

20 Yes, •and however many the promises God (C4) made, the Yes to them all is in him. That is why it is "through him" that we answer

21 Amen to the praise of God. •Remember it is God himself who assures us all, and you, of our standing in Christ, and has anointed

22 us, •marking us with his seal and giving us the pledge, the Spirit, that we carry in our hearts.

23   By my life, I call God to witness that the reason why I did not come to Corinth after (C3)

24 all was to spare your feelings. •We are not dictators over your faith, but are fellow workers with you for your happiness; in the faith

1 you are steady enough. 2 Well then, I (C4) made up my mind not to pay you a second (C3) 2 distressing visit. ·I may have hurt you, but if so I have hurt the only people who could give 3 me any pleasure. ·I wrote as I did to make sure that, when I came, I should not be distressed by the very people who should have (C3) made me happy. I am sure you all know that I could never be happy unless you were. 4 When I wrote to you, in deep distress and anguish of mind, and in tears, it was not to make you feel hurt but to let you know how much love I have for you. (C3)

5 Someone has been the cause of pain; and the cause of pain not to me, but to some (C2) degree—not to overstate it—to all of you. 6 The punishment already imposed by the ma- (C3) jority on the man in question is enough; 7 and the best thing now is to give him your forgiveness and encouragement, or he might (C3) 8 break down from so much misery. ·So I am (C3) asking you to give some definite proof of 9 your love for him. ·What I really wrote for, after all, was to test you and see whether you (C3) 10 are completely obedient. ·Anybody that you (C3) forgive, I forgive; and as for my forgiving anything—if there has been anything to be forgiven, I have forgiven it for your sake in (C3) 11 the presence of Christ. ·And so we will not be outwitted by Satan—we know well enough what his intentions are.

From Troas to Macedonia. The apostolate: its importance

12 When I went up to Troas to preach the (C3) Good News of Christ, and the door was wide 13 open for my work there in the Lord, ·I was so continually uneasy in mind at not meeting brother Titus there, I said good-bye to them and went on to Macedonia.

14 Thanks be to God who, wherever he goes, makes us, in Christ, partners of his triumph,*a* (C3) and through us is spreading the knowledge

114

of himself, like a sweet smell, everywhere.
15 We are Christ's incense to God for those who (C3)
are being saved and for those who are not;
16 for the last, the smell of death that leads to
death, for the first the sweet smell of life that
leads to life. And who could be qualified for
17 work like this? •At least we do not go round
offering the word of God for sale, as many (C2)
other people do. In Christ, we speak as men (C3)
of sincerity, as envoys of God and in God's
presence.

Week 2 Day 1
Four C's Meditations
on 2 Corinthians 1:1-2:17

1. Jesus, our meditation today overflows
with expressions of St. Paul's tender love for
his spiritual children at Corinth. This contrasts
sharply with the sternness displayed in his first
letter. Yet both epistles reveal genuine seed-
charity. *(Be sure to read the introductory remarks on 2
Corinthians found in paragraphs 63-66 of the Introduction to this book.)*

2. St. Paul was stern only as a means of
bringing his erring children back to the way of
truth. But now that the necessary corrections

115

were made, a relieved and grateful Paul gives way to tenderness. Thus, we see in Paul two manifestations of his sacrificial love.

3.   In Second Corinthians, St. Paul addresses himself to the subject of suffering.[40] He writes to console the Corinthians in their distress, and he refers as well to the sufferings he and his companions gladly endured for the spread of the Good News of salvation.

4.   We noted, too, that St. Paul also calls these torments Your sufferings, that is, sufferings experienced in Your Mystical Body, the Church. We see this idea expressed elsewhere as well, when he wrote: "It makes me happy to suffer for you, as I am suffering now, and in my own body to do what I can to make up all that has still to be undergone by Christ for the sake of His body, the Church."[41]

5.   In Your plan of salvation, Lord, suffering has an important role to play. Offered as an expression of seed-charity, it serves to further the spread of Your Church on earth and to increase the sanctity of its members. We suffer for Your sake when we try to avoid sin. We also suffer for Your sake when we deliberately choose to do what is difficult out of our love for You and for our fellow Christians and for those who have not yet received the Faith. *(For more on the value of suffering, see "The Catholic Catechism," pp. 430-432.)*

6.   You, of course, Most Blessed Lord, are the supreme example of voluntary suffering

116

for the sake of others. When we suffer for Your sake and for the sake of others, we know You have preceded us in agony, but to a degree very few have even come close to equaling.

7. We know too that when we suffer as Your followers and friends, You will console us. "Come to me, all who labor and are over-burdened, and I will give you rest. Shoulder my yoke and learn from me, for I am gentle and humble in heart, and you will find rest for your souls. Yes, my yoke is easy and my burden light."[42]

8. Most Sacred Heart of Jesus, St. Paul experienced Your promised consolation when he wrote, "Indeed, as the sufferings of Christ overflow to us, so, through Christ, does our consolation overflow."[43] And again, "Blessed be God the Father of Our Lord Jesus Christ, a gentle Father and the God of all consolation, who comforts us in all our sorrows."[44]

9. This does not mean, Lord, that we will always experience Your consolations at the precise moment we suffer for Your sake. You Yourself, for example, experienced a sense of excruciating abandonment when You were dying on the Cross for us. Yet, You also knew the Father was actually with You, but not in a manner that could be physically sensed.

10. We can also contrast suffering for Your sake with the suffering which follows sin. In the case of the latter, there may be momentary pleasure and satisfaction which

117

precedes the suffering, but real joy, peace and happiness are never found. A person who becomes addicted to sin is always an unhappy person, whereas those who suffer the most for Your sake, Lord, are the happiest of persons. We speak, of course, of Your saints. Thus, it follows that those who persist in Christian suffering until death are rewarded with Heaven, while those who persist in their sins until death having hardened their hearts, are eternally punished in hell.

11. Jesus, divine Savior, by the power of Your Holy Spirit constantly inspire us to resist all temptations to sin. Thus, we will be aided in preventing the devil from gaining more power over ourselves, our families, our country and the entire world. Moreover, Lord, inspire us not to be content with only resisting sin. That is, inspire us to choose to perform all our responsibilities in the most perfect way possible, for the sake of Your Name. Inspire us to live a life of atonement so we can be used as instruments to increase Your reign over the world. Inspire us to pray with deeper fervor, to receive Your sacra-

ments with deeper fervor, and to fervently love You in our neighbor.

12. We noted too, Lord, in our reading, the severe punishment of excommunication ordered by St. Paul for the man living sinfully with his stepmother had the desired effect of repentance. Consequently, Paul compassionately writes, "The punishment already imposed by the majority on the man in question is enough; and the best thing now is to give him your forgiveness and encouragement, or he might break down from so much misery. So I am asking you to give some definite proof of your love for him."[45]

13. This incident reminds us, Jesus, of the responsibilities parents have for the welfare of their children. May they never be afraid to discipline them when they need it, but without losing control of their temper. Failing to discipline them would really be a sin against charity, since it would be neglecting to do what is best for them. On the other hand, once it has been administered, may parents express their love for their children with affection and tenderness.

14. Lord, this responsibility brings to mind the following prayer of a parent addressed to Mary.

15. "Our Lady of Providence, My Queen and My Mother, to You I confide the children God has entrusted to me. Now while they are small provide for their safety of body, mind, and heart; tomorrow when I shall no longer be with them, when the responsibilities and

greater temptations of life shall be theirs, then, My Lady, for my sons and daughters continue to be the Mother of Providence.

16. "Above all, My Queen, be with my children when the angel of death hovers near, and in the arms of Thy Loving Providence, I beseech You, take my children into eternity that forever and ever they may praise the Father, the Son and Holy Spirit. Amen."

Try to re-read and re-meditate on these Scripture passages and reflections at least one more time today.

Please read and meditate on Chapter III, Paragraphs 61 to 70 in our "Prayers and Recommended Practices" book.

WEEK 2 DAY 2
2 Corinthians 3:1-4:18

1 3 Does this sound like a new attempt to commend ourselves to you? Unlike other people, we need no letters of recommenda-
2 tion either to you or from you, ·because you are yourselves our letter, written in our
3 hearts, that anybody can see and read, ·and

it is plain that you are a letter from Christ, drawn up by us, and written not with ink but with the Spirit of the living God, not on stone tablets but on the tablets of your living hearts.

4 Before God, we are confident of this (C4)
5 through Christ: •not that we are qualified in ourselves to claim anything as our own work:
6 all our qualifications come from God. •He is the one who has given us the qualifications to be the administrators of this new covenant, which is not a covenant of written letters but of the Spirit: the written letters bring death,
7 but the Spirit gives life. •Now if the administering of death, in the written letters engraved on stones, was accompanied by such a brightness that the Israelites could not bear looking at the face of Moses, though it was a bright-
8 ness that faded, •then how much greater will be the brightness that surrounds the adminis-
9 tering of the Spirit! •For if there was any splendor in administering condemnation, there must be very much greater splendor in
10 administering justification. •In fact, compared with this greater splendor, the thing that used to have such splendor now seems to have
11 none; •and if what was so temporary had any splendor, there must be much more in what is going to last for ever.

12 Having this hope, we can be quite confi- (C1)
13 dent; •not like Moses, who put a veil over his face so that the Israelites would not notice
14 the ending of what had to fade.*a* •And anyway, their minds had been dulled; indeed, to this very day, that same veil is still there when the old covenant is being read, a veil never
15 lifted, since Christ alone can remove it. •Yes, even today, whenever Moses is read, the veil
16 is over their minds. •It will not be removed
17 until they turn to the Lord. •Now this Lord (C1) is the Spirit, and where the Spirit of the Lord (C2)
18 is, there is freedom. •And we, with our un- (C3) veiled faces reflecting like mirrors the bright- ness of the Lord, all grow brighter and brighter (C4)

121

as we are turned into the image that we reflect; this is the work of the Lord who is Spirit.

4 1 Since we have by an act of mercy been entrusted with this work of administration, (C3) 2 there is no weakening on our part. •On the (C4) contrary, we will have none of the reticence of those who are ashamed, no deceitfulness (C2) or watering down the word of God; but the way we commend ourselves to every human (C2) being with a conscience is by stating the truth (C3) 3 openly in the sight of God. •If our gospel does not penetrate the veil, then the veil is (C2) on those who are not on the way to salvation; 4 the unbelievers whose minds the god of this world has blinded, to stop them seeing the light shed by the Good News of the glory of 5 Christ, who is the image of God. •For it is not ourselves that we are preaching, but (C3) Christ Jesus as the Lord, and ourselves as 6 your servants for Jesus' sake. •It is the same God that said, "Let there be light shining out of darkness," who has shone in our minds to radiate the light of the knowledge of God's glory, the glory on the face of Christ.

The trials and hopes of the apostolate

7 We are only the earthenware jars that hold this treasure, to make it clear that such an overwhelming power comes from God and (C4) 8 not from us. ·We are in difficulties on all sides, but never cornered; we see no an-

9 swer to our problems, but never despair; ·we (C4) have been persecuted, but never deserted; 10 knocked down, but never killed; ·always, wherever we may be, we carry with us in our (C2) body the death of Jesus, so that the life of (C4) Jesus, too, may always be seen in our body. 11 Indeed, while we are still alive, we are con- (C3) signed to our death every day, for the sake of Jesus, so that in our mortal flesh the life 12 of Jesus, too, may be openly shown. ·So death is at work in us, but life in you.

13 But as we have the same spirit of faith that (C1) is mentioned in scripture—*I believed, and therefore I spoke*[a]—we too believe and there- (C1) 14 fore we too speak, ·knowing that he who raised the Lord Jesus to life will raise us with Jesus in our turn, and put us by his side and 15 you with us. ·You see, all this is for your (C3) benefit, so that the more grace is multiplied among people, the more thanksgiving there will be, to the glory of God.

16 That is why there is no weakening on our part, and instead, though this outer man of ours may be falling into decay, the inner man (C4) 17 is renewed day by day. ·Yes, the troubles which are soon over, though they weigh little, train us for the carrying of a weight of eternal

glory which is out of all proportion to them. 18 And so we have no eyes for things that are visible, but only for things that are invisible; for visible things last only for a time, and the invisible things are eternal.

123

Week 2 Day 2
Four C's Meditations
on 2 Corinthians 3:1-4:18

1. Jesus, Our Lord and Our God, how important it is to have faith and hope in You! If we do not, salvation cannot be ours.

2. With the theological virtue of faith we can believe the truths which we must know for our salvation. And with the theological virtue of hope we can trust in You and have the hope of eternal life in Your heavenly Kingdom.[46]

3. In today's meditation, Lord, we noted in particular that St. Paul was using Your gift of faith.[47] Only through faith was he able to accept the truth that the New Covenant, unlike the Old, is a covenant of the Holy Spirit giving eternal life to its adherents.[48] Furthermore, St. Paul states that because Christianity is a covenant of the Spirit, Christians, with the Spirit's aid, can reflect "like mirrors the brightness of the Lord (and) all grow brighter and brighter as we are turned into the image that we reflect. . . ."[49]

4.   It is also through Your Holy Spirit, Lord, that we are given seed-charity, the greatest of Your theological virtues, so we can become increasingly like You. Therefore, in humility, we ask You to help us avoid all sin, especially mortal sin, so that Your Holy Spirit and seed-charity will always be with us.

5.   Reflecting on today's reading, Lord we also learned an important lesson from St. Paul with respect to sharing the Gospel with others. He revealed that when he and his co-workers evangelized, they did so without deceit, and without watering down Your Good News of salvation. Instead, they spoke boldly, "stating the truth openly in the sight of God."[50]

6.   Essentially then, St. Paul is saying that when we share the Faith we must not be ashamed or fearful. Moreover, we must be confident that You will accompany us in this work as You have promised.[51]

7.   Unfortunately, Jesus, we must admit that

at times we are fearful and ashamed to share Your words of everlasting life with others. One wonders if this isn't due largely to the influence of satan, who spares no effort in preventing the salvation of souls.

8. Lord, help us to share Your words with others, so that they too may have access to You and Your gift of salvation. May we do so openly and without shame, fear or deceit.

9. Most Sacred Heart of Jesus, we noticed the many painful trials St. Paul and his companions experienced in their efforts to bring others to You. What confidence, charity and constancy they must have had to accomplish their goal! What pure consciences they must have had to be sensitive to the inspirations of Your Holy Spirit!

10. Addressing himself to the difficulties he encountered in evangelizing, St. Paul wrote, "Yes, the troubles which are soon over, though they weigh little, train us for the carrying of a weight of eternal glory which is out of all proportion to them."[52]

11. St. Peter also wrote similiar words.

12. "My dear people, you must not think it unaccountable that you should be tested by fire. There is nothing extraordinary in what has happened to you. If you can have some share in the sufferings of Christ, be glad, because you will enjoy a much greater gladness when his glory is revealed. It is a blessing for you when they insult you for bearing the name of Christ, because it means

that you have the Spirit of glory, the Spirit of God resting on you."[(53)]

13.   Lord, grant us the courage to be willing to suffer, if that is what is necessary to bring others to salvation. We know, too, that those who suffer for You and the sake of the Gospel will be greatly rewarded. Amen.

The more you re-read these Scriptures and meditations, the more you will get out of them.

Please read and meditate on Chapter IV, Paragraphs 1 to 26 in our "Prayers and Recommended Practices" book.

WEEK 2 DAY 3
2 Corinthians 5:1-6:18

1 5 For we know that when the tent that we live in on earth is folded up, there is a house built by God for us, an everlasting home not made by human hands, in the heav-
2 ens. ·In this present state, it is true, we groan as we wait with longing to put on our heav- (C1)
3 enly home over the other; ·we should like to be found wearing clothes and not without

4 them. ·Yes, we groan and find it a burden being still in this tent, not that we want to strip it off, but to put the second garment over it and to have what must die taken up into life. (C3)
5 This is the purpose for which God made us, and he has given us the pledge of the Spirit.
6 We are always full of confidence, then, when we remember that to live in the body (C1)
7 means to be exiled from the Lord, ·going as (C1)
8 we do by faith and not by sight ·—we are full of confidence, I say, and actually want to be exiled from the body and make our home (C1)
9 with the Lord. ·Whether we are living in the body or exiled from it, we are intent on pleas- (C2)
10 ing him. ·For all the truth about us will be brought out in the law court of Christ, and each of us will get what he deserves for the things he did in the body, good or bad. (C3) (C3) (C2)

The apostolate in action

11 And so it is with the fear of the Lord in mind that we try to win people over. God knows us for what we really are, and I hope that in your consciences you know us too. (C3) (C2)
12 This is not another attempt to commend ourselves to you: we are simply giving you reasons to be proud of us, so that you will have an answer ready for the people who can boast more about what they seem than what they (C3) (C2)
13 are. ·If we seemed out of our senses, it was for God; but if we are being reasonable now,
14 it is for your sake. ·And this is because the love of Christ overwhelms us when we reflect that if one man has died for all, then all men (C3)
15 should be dead; ·and the reason he died for all was so that living men should live no longer for themselves, but for him who died and was raised to life for them. (C2) (C3)
16 From now onward, therefore, we do not judge anyone by the standards of the flesh. Even if we did once know Christ in the flesh, (C2)
17 that is not how we know him now. ·And for anyone who is in Christ, there is a new crea-

128

tion; the old creation has gone, and now the
18 new one is here. •It is all God's work. It was
God who reconciled us to himself through
Christ and gave us the work of handing on
19 this reconciliation. •In other words, God in (C3)
Christ was reconciling the world to himself, (C2)
not holding men's faults against them, and he
has entrusted to us the news that they are (C3)
20 reconciled. •So we are ambassadors for
Christ; it is as though God were appealing
through us, and the appeal that we make in (C3)
21 Christ's name is: be reconciled to God. •For
our sake God made the sinless one into sin,
so that in him we might become the goodness (C3)
1 of God. 6 As his fellow workers, we beg
you once again not to neglect the grace of (C2)
2 God that you have received. •For he says: *At
the favorable time, I have listened to you; on
the day of salvation I came to your help.*[a]
Well, now is the favorable time; this is the day
of salvation.

3   We do nothing that people might object to, (C3)
so as not to bring discredit on our function
4 as God's servants. •Instead, we prove we are (C4)
servants of God by great fortitude in times

of suffering: in times of hardship and distress;
5 when we are flogged, or sent to prison, or (C3)
6 mobbed; laboring, sleepless, starving. ·We
prove we are God's servants by our purity, (C2)
knowledge, patience and kindness; by a spirit
of holiness, by a love free from affectation; (C3)
7 by the word of truth and by the power of
God; by being armed with the weapons of
righteousness in the right hand and in the left, (C3)
8 prepared for honor or disgrace, for blame or
praise; taken for impostors while we are
9 genuine; ·obscure yet famous; said to be dying and here are we alive; rumored to be
10 executed before we are sentenced; ·thought
most miserable and yet we are always rejoic- (C3)
ing; taken for paupers though we make others (C3)
rich, for people having nothing though we
have everything.

Paul opens his heart. A warning

11   Corinthians, we have spoken to you very
frankly; our mind has been opened in front
12 of you. ·Any constraint that you feel is not

on our side; the constraint is in your own (C2)
13 selves. ·I speak as if to children of mine: as
a fair exchange, open your minds in the same
way.

14   Do not harness yourselves in an uneven (C2)
team with unbelievers. Virtue is no companion for crime. Light and darkness have noth- (C1)
15 ing in common. ·Christ is not the ally of
Beliar, nor has a believer anything to share
16 with an unbeliever. ·The temple of God has (C2)
no common ground with idols, and that is
what we are—the temple of the living God. (C2)
We have God's word for it: *I will make my
home among them and live with them; I will
be their God and they shall be my people.b*
17 Then *come away from them and keep aloof,* (C3)
says the Lord. Touch nothing that is unclean,c
18 *and I will welcome you ·and be your father,*
and you shall be my sons and daughters, says
the Almighty Lord.d

Week 2 Day 3
Four C's Meditations
on 2 Corinthians 5:1-6:18

1. Lord, we learned today that St. Paul passionately longed to be with You, body and soul, in Heaven. [54] Oh that we might have that same longing for unending happiness and joy.

2. Sadly, many of us find this world of time and space so attractive that our thoughts are seldom on eternity. And this is true in spite of unending trials and difficulties in this life.

3. Of course, it isn't wrong to enjoy the world which You have made for us. But when compared to eternity and the joys that await us, life on earth is seen to be a relatively small and inferior part of Your plan for mankind.

4. You said something once, Lord, that sums up what we wish to convey here. "Anyone who prefers father or mother to me is not worthy of me. Anyone who prefers son or daughter to me is not worthy of me." [55] In

131

other words, nothing on earth, no matter how good and lovable, is to take first place to You. You, Lord, and not our loved ones, or the other things You have created, are the Source of all goodness and all happiness and all joy. And since we will find our fullest happiness and joy with You only in Heaven, it makes sense to long to be there with You, body and soul. Jesus, grant us an ardent desire to be with You in Heaven where we will see You "face to face" and receive the rewards of faithful discipleship. But until the time comes when You will call us to our eternal destiny, grant us the necessary faith, trust and love to serve You well on earth.

5. Lord, there are also those who long to "end it all" because of hardships and tragedies they have encountered on earth. But this is a far cry from St. Paul's yearning to be with You in Heaven. Actually, their longing reflects their desperation, i.e., their lack of confidence in Your loving providence over their lives, and their lack of faith that You will forgive even the worst of sinners.

6. We must believe that when things are difficult, you will see us through them, if we trust and love You. The difficulties of life which we encounter constitute the crosses we must bear, if we are to be Your loyal disciples. As St. Paul said in our previous meditation, "Yes, the troubles which are soon over, though they weigh little, train us for the carrying of a weight of eternal glory which is out of proportion to them."[56]

7. Most Sacred Heart of Jesus, may we always have the necessary confidence in You to see us through the troubles and crises of our earthly pilgrimage.

8. Lord, St. Paul also refers in today's meditation to the rewards and punishments You give according to our conduct in this life.[57] We know that if we persevere to the end in planting seeds of supernatural charity, You will eternally reward us. On the other hand, if we fail to exercise seed-charity and therefore sin, we are liable to punishment, whether in this life or in Purgatory, or in hell.

9. Thankfully, Lord, through the sacrament of penance we can avoid the eternal punishment of hell. This sacrament truly reflects Your immense love for us. We can also avoid much, if not all, of the punishment due us in Purgatory by works of penance in this life which are also works of seed-charity. We can even, through various acts of penance, merit increases of sanctifying grace for others, including those in Purgatory. *(For more on penance and its relationship to indulgences, see "The Catholic Catechism," pp. 555-562.)*

10. Next, Jesus, our attention focused in our meditation on St. Paul's expression of thanksgiving for Your sacrificial death for us on the Cross.

11. "The love of Christ overwhelms us when we reflect that if one man had died for all, then all men should be dead; and the reason he died for all was so that living men

should live no longer for themselves, but for him who died and was raised up for them."(58)

12.   Your supreme act of seed-charity, Lord, was Your voluntary death on our behalf. This unmatched act of self-denial is our model and incentive for dying to selfishness and living for others with acts of self-sacrificing love. Thus we are following in Your footsteps of self-sacrifice when we seek the well-being and salvation of others. Moreover, we are fostering salvation for ourselves in the process. Lord, inspire us to model our lives after You, Your Blessed Mother, St. Joseph and all the saints, thereby winning many souls for Heaven and also preparing a place for ourselves.

13.   Jesus, Our Lord, St. Paul also begged the Corinthian Christians, "not to neglect the grace of God" they had received.(59) This statement serves to remind us that we are only cooperators with You in the process of our salvation and sanctification. We could neither be saved nor become holy without the

grace You charitably merited for us throughout Your life on earth, but especially when You suffered and died on the Cross. And You have ordained too that our salvation and sanctification depend on how well we use the grace You have freely merited for us.

14. Finally, St. Paul emphasized the fact that he and his companions made every effort to avoid giving occasions of scandal so that the spreading of the Good News of salvation might not be hindered.[60] These efforts included continuous acts of confidence during times of unjust punishment. They also consisted in acts of seed-charity which were reflected in such virtues as purity, patience and kindness under the most adverse circumstances.

15. Lord, how important virtuous living is in attracting others to You! Every day, we should allow You to shine like a beacon through our lives, thus drawing others to You. But how often we fail, because of our sins, to let You do this. Please forgive us. Keep us in Your friendship and inspire us to grow in grace so we can become more effective instruments of Your saving love. Amen.

We hope that you will find time to re-read and re-meditate on the Scripture reading for today, and, in doing so, may the Holy Spirit give you His gift of peace which the world cannot give.

Please read and meditate on Chapter IV, Paragraphs 27-43 in our "Prayers and Recommended Practices" book.

WEEK 2 DAY 4
2 Corinthians 7:1-9:15

1 7With promises like these made to us, dear
brothers, let us wash off all that can soil (C2)
either body or spirit, to reach perfection of
holiness in the fear of God.

2 Keep a place for us in your hearts. We have (C3)
not injured anyone, or ruined anyone, or ex- (C2)
3 ploited anyone. ·I am not saying this to put
any blame on you; as I have already told you,
you are in our hearts—together we live or
4 together we die. ·I have the very greatest
confidence in you, and I am so proud of you
that in all our trouble I am filled with consola- (C3)
tion and my joy is overflowing.

Paul in Macedonia; he is joined by Titus

5 Even after we had come to Macedonia,
however, there was no rest for this body of
ours. Far from it; we found trouble on all (C2)
sides: quarrels outside, misgivings inside.
6 But God comforts the miserable, and he
7 comforted us, by the arrival of Titus, ·and not
only by his arrival but also by the comfort
which he had gained from you. He has told ′ ³⁾
us all about how you want to see me, how

sorry you were, and how concerned for me, and so I am happier now than I was before. 8 But to tell the truth, even if I distressed you by my letter, I do not regret it. I did (c3) regret it before, and I see that that letter did 9 distress you, at least for a time; •but I am happy now—not because I made you suffer, but because your suffering led to your repent- (c2)

ance. Yours has been a kind of suffering that God approves, and so you have come to no 10 kind of harm from us. •To suffer in God's (c3) way means changing for the better and leaves no regrets, but to suffer as the world knows (c2) 11 suffering brings death. •Just look at what suf- fering in God's way has brought you: what keenness, what explanations, what indigna- tion, what alarm! Yes, and what aching to see (c3) me, what concern for me, and what justice done! In every way you have shown your- 12 selves blameless in this affair. •So then, (c2) though I wrote the letter to you, it was not written for the sake either of the offender or of the one offended; it was to make you real- ize, in the sight of God, your own concern (c3) 13 for us. •That is what we have found so en- couraging.

With this encouragement, too, we had the even greater happiness of finding Titus so happy; thanks to you all, he has no more (c3)

14 worries; •I had rather boasted to him about you, and now I have not been made to look foolish; in fact, our boasting to Titus has proved to be as true as anything that we ever 15 said to you. •His own personal affection for (C3) you is all the greater when he remembers how willing you have all been, and with what 16 deep respect you welcomed him. •I am very (C3) happy knowing that I can rely on you so completely.

II. ORGANIZATION OF THE COLLECTION

Why the Corinthians should be generous

1 8 Now here, brothers, is the news of the grace of God which was given in the 2 churches in Macedonia; •and of how, (C3) throughout great trials by suffering, their constant cheerfulness and their intense pov- (C4) erty have overflowed in a wealth of gen- (C3) 3 erosity. •I can swear that they gave not only as much as they could afford, but far more, 4 and quite spontaneously, •begging and beg- (C3) ging us for the favor of sharing in this service 5 to the saints •and, what was quite unexpected, (C3) they offered their own selves first to God and, under God, to us. (C3)

6 Because of this, we have asked Titus, since he has already made a beginning, to bring this work of mercy to the same point of success 7 among you. •You always have the most of (CI) everything—of faith, of eloquence, of understanding, of keenness for any cause, and the biggest share of our affection—so we expect (C3) you to put the most into this work of mercy (C3) 8 too. •It is not an order that I am giving you; I am just testing the genuineness of your love (C3) 9 against the keenness of others. •Remember how generous the Lord Jesus was: he was rich, but he became poor for your sake, to 10 make you rich out of his poverty. •As I say,

I am only making a suggestion; it is only fair to you, since you were the first, a year ago, not only in taking action but even in deciding

11 to. ·So now finish the work and let the results (C3) be worthy, as far as you can afford it, of the

12 decision you made so promptly. ·As long as the readiness is there, a man is acceptable with whatever he can afford; never mind what

13 is beyond his means. ·This does not mean that to give relief to others you ought to make (C3) things difficult for yourselves: it is a question

14 of balancing ·what happens to be your surplus now against their present need, and one day they may have something to spare that (C3) will supply your own need. That is how we

15 strike a balance: ·as scripture says: *The man who gathered much had none too much, the man who gathered little did not go short.*[a]

16 I thank God for putting into Titus' heart (C3)
the same concern for you that I have myself.
17 He did what we asked him; indeed he is more (C3)
concerned than ever, and is visiting you on
18 his own initiative. ·As his companion we are
sending the brother who is famous in all the
19 churches for spreading the gospel. ·More
than that, he happens to be the same brother
who has been elected by the churches to be
our companion on this errand of mercy that,
for the glory of God, we have undertaken to (C3)
20 satisfy our impatience to help. ·We hope that
in this way there will be no accusations made
about our administering such a large fund;
21 for *we are trying to do right* not only *in the
sight of God* but *also* in the sight of *men.*[b] (C3)
22 To accompany these, we are sending a third
brother, of whose keenness we have often
had proof in many different ways, and who
is particularly keen about this, because he has
23 great confidence in you. ·Titus, perhaps I
should add, is my own colleague and fellow

worker in your interests; the other two brothers, who are delegates of the churches, are
24 a real glory to Christ. ·So then, in front of
all the churches, give them a proof of your (C3)
love, and prove to them that we are right to
be proud of you.

1 **9** There is really no need for me to write to
you on the subject of offering your serv-
2 ices to the saints, ·since I know how anxious (C3)
you are to help; in fact, I boast about you to
the Macedonians, telling them, "Achaia has
been ready since last year." So your zeal has (C3)
3 been a spur to many more. ·I am sending the
brothers all the same, to make sure that our
boasting about you does not prove to have
been empty this time, and that you really are
4 ready as I said you would be. ·If some of the (C3)
Macedonians who are coming with me found
you unprepared, we should be humiliated

140

—to say nothing of yourselves—after being
5 so confident. ·That is why I have thought it
necessary to ask these brothers to go on to
you ahead of us, and make sure in advance
that the gift you promised is all ready, and
that it all comes as a gift out of your
generosity and not by being extorted from (C3)
you.

Blessings to be expected from the collection

6   Do not forget: thin sowing means thin
reaping; the more you sow, the more you (C3)
7 reap. ·Each one should give what he has decided in his own mind, not grudgingly or
because he is made to, for *God loves a cheer-* (C3)
8 *ful giver.*ᵃ ·And there is no limit to the blessings which God can send you—he will
make sure that you will always have all you
need for yourselves in every possible
circumstance, and still have something to
9 spare for all sorts of good works. ·As scripture says: *He was free in almsgiving, and* (C3)
*gave to the poor: his good deeds will never
be forgotten.*ᵇ

10   The one who provides *seed for the sower* (C3)
and bread for food will provide you with all
the seed you want and make *the harvest of* (C3)
11 *your good deeds* a larger one, ·and, made
richer in every way, you will be able to do
all the generous things which, through us, are (C3)
12 the cause of thanksgiving to God. ·For doing
this holy service is not only supplying all the
needs of the saints, but it is also increasing (C3)
the amount of· thanksgiving that God re (C3)
13 ceives. ·By offering this service, you show (C3)
them what you are, and that makes them give
glory to God for the way you accept and (C3)
profess the gospel of Christ, and for your (C3)
sympathetic generosity to them and to all. (C3)
14 And their prayers for you, too, show how
they are drawn to you on account of all the
15 grace that God has given you. ·Thanks be to (C3)
God for his inexpressible gift!

141

Week 2 Day 4
Four C's Meditations
on 2 Corinthians 7:1-9:15

1. Lord, at the very beginning of today's meditation St. Paul writes that to obtain perfection in holiness everything that can stain the body and the soul must be removed. [61] This, of course, refers to the whole spectrum of sins which prevent us from fully serving You.

2. Of course, it is not our fault as individuals that sin entered the world. Nor is it our fault that we were conceived and born apart from Your friendship. But it is our fault when we fail to do something about our own sinfulness and the temptations to sin which continually harass us.

3. Thankfully, we can be forgiven both our venial and mortal sins through Your sacrament of Confession. Moreover, we can be forgiven our venial sins even apart from Confession. And by means of prayer and the

grace of the sacraments, we receive Your help to combat temptations which arise from within our beings and from without. We are grateful too that Your Holy Catholic Church teaches us what is sinful and cautions us to avoid occasions of sin. *(For the advantages of confessing venial sins in the Sacrament of Confession, read pp. 495-497 of "The Catholic Catechism.")*

4.   Blessed Lord, constantly inspire us to avoid sin at all costs, even venial sins, so we may perfectly serve You and others in this life and in the life to come.

5.   Jesus, Redeemer of souls, in one of our earlier readings, St. Paul mentioned the need of contributions for the Church in Jerusalem.[62] In today's reading, he continues with his appeal, indicating how the collection will not only benefit the recipients in Jerusalem but also the benefactors from Corinth and elsewhere.[63]

6.   Before making his solicitation, however, Paul noted the generosity and cheerfulness of the Christians in Macedonia, who despite many trials and extreme poverty gave liberally to the Jerusalem Church. This reminds us of the widow You mentioned in St. Luke's Gospel who, in spite of her poverty, gave all she had for the needs of others.[64] *(Read also I Kings 17:7-24 where a widow, during a drought, shared with the prophet Elijah her last portion of food. Yet for this act of sacrifice, God provided her and her son with meal and oil until the drought was over.)*

7.   This type of giving reveals not only charity, but also tremendous belief and trust in

God; belief and trust that God will meet the continuing needs of all who unreservedly surrender themselves to Him.

8. Lord, teach us to be more generous, not only with our money and material goods, but also with our time. Inspire us to spend more time in praying for others and in comforting the sick, the sorrowing and others who experience difficult situations, particularly members of our own families. Also inspire us to be more generous in the use of all the talents, natural and supernatural, that You have so generously given us. We realize too, Lord, that one day we will have to render an accounting for these gifts.

9. Jesus, St. Paul also reminded the Corinthians in his appeal for their support, how richly You had blessed them. Thus in gratitude for such charity, he urged them to give sacrificially for the Jerusalem Christians. He also stressed that their help should be given freely and not as if they were compelled to do it, since charity, if it is genuine, Lord, is always given freely.[65]

10.   Lord, we were particularly impressed by the words St. Paul used to describe Your love, not only for the Corinthians but for all men. Certainly, the faithful in Corinth were moved by them. "He was rich, but he became poor for your sake, to make you rich out of his poverty."[66] Yes, Jesus, You Who own the entire universe, in order to make us eternally rich in sanctity, humbled Yourself to become a poor man of Nazareth and to die the death of a criminal at the hands of Your creatures. How unworthy we are of such love!

11.   Returning now to the subject of the collection to be made on behalf of the Jerusalem Christians, St. Paul actually did not counsel the Corinthians to make extraordinary sacrifices. "As long as the readiness is there, a man is acceptable with whatever he can afford."[67]

12.   From these words, Lord, we learn that our acts of seed-charity should be governed by the supernatural virtue of prudence. We should not, however, deceive ourselves by equating stinginess with prudence. No, prudential giving should always be sacrificial giving. But normally this does not require giving away what is absolutely necessary to maintain the lives and health of ourselves and families. *(For more on seed-charity, see "The Catholic Catechism," pp. 193-194; 197-200.)*

13.   Still, there are those heroic souls, such as the poor widows mentioned above, who have such confidence in You that they give even from their necessity, being confident that

145

You will supply whatever is lacking in their needs. And experience shows that You indeed do so, time and time again. We might say that this type of giving is also prudential, since those exercising it know from experience that You will supply them with whatever is necessary.

14. This certainly was the case with St. Paul himself. He constantly gave of himself for others, often seeking no compensation from them. Yet he was confident that You would always meet his needs, and You always did.

15. Lord, in his concluding remarks in chapter ten, St. Paul stresses the rewards of seed-charity which are given in direct proportion to the sacrifices we make. "Thin sowing means thin reaping; the more you sow, the more you reap."[68] And for those who plant seeds of charity, "...there is no limit to the blessings which God can send you — he will make sure that you will always have all you need for yourselves in every possible circumstance, and still have something to spare for all sorts of good works."[69]

16. Lord, may we never waver or tire in performing works of mercy, especially those works directed towards the spiritual well-being of those You bring into our lives, particularly members of our own families. Constantly remind us that You will always reward us for our generosity, including the priceless rewards of interior peace, happiness and joy. We praise You, Lord, for all of Your kindness to us and to all men. Amen.

Try to read these Scripture passages and meditations several times a day in a reflective manner. Each time you do so, the Holy Spirit will give you more insights.

Please read and meditate on Chapter IV, Paragraphs 44 to 53 in our "Prayers and Recommended Practices" book.

WEEK 2 DAY 5
2 Corinthians 10:1-11:33

III. PAUL'S APOLOGIA

Paul's reply to accusations of weakness

1 **10** This is a personal matter; this is Paul (C3) himself appealing to you by the gentle-

ness and patience of Christ—I, the man who is so humble when he is facing you, but bullies you when he is at a distance. •I only ask that I do not have to bully you when I come, with all the confident assurance I mean to show when I come face to face with people I could name who think we go by ordinary human motives. •We live in the flesh, of course, but the muscles that we fight with are not flesh. •Our war is not fought with weapons of flesh, yet they are strong enough, in God's cause, to demolish fortresses. We demolish sophistries, •and the arrogance that (C2) tries to resist the knowledge of God; every thought is our prisoner, captured to be brought into obedience to Christ. •Once you have given your complete obedience, we are (C3) prepared to punish any disobedience.

7 Face plain facts. Anybody who is con- (C1) vinced that he belongs to Christ must go on to reflect that we all belong to Christ no less than he does. •Maybe I do boast rather too much about our authority, but the Lord gave it to me for building you up and not for pull- (C3) ing you down, and I shall not be ashamed of (C1) it. •I do not want you to think of me as someone who only frightens you by letter. •Someone said, "He writes powerful and strongly-worded letters but when he is with you you see only half a man and no preacher at all." The man who said that can remember this: whatever we are like in the words of our letters when we are absent, that is what we shall be like in our actions when we are present.

His reply to the accusation of ambition

12 We are not being so bold as to rank ourselves, or invite comparison, with certain peo- (C2) ple who write their own references. Measuring themselves against themselves, and comparing themselves to themselves, they are simply foolish. •We, on the other hand,

are not going to boast without a standard to
measure against: taking for our measure the
yardstick which God gave us to measure
with, which is long enough to reach to you.
14 We are not stretching further than we ought;
otherwise we should not have reached you,
as we did come all the way to you with the
15 gospel of Christ. •So we are not boasting (C3)
without any measure, about work that was (C3)
done by other people; in fact, we trust that, (C1)
as your faith grows, we shall get taller and
16 taller, when judged by our own standard. •I
mean, we shall be carrying the gospel to (C2)
places far beyond you, without encroaching
on anyone else's field, not boasting of the
17 work already done. •*If anyone wants to boast,*
18 *let him boast of the Lord.*ᵃ •It is not the man (C2)
who commends himself that can be accepted,
but the man who is commended by the Lord.

Paul is driven to sound his own praises

1 **11** I only wish you were able to tolerate
a little foolishness from me. But of
2 course: you are tolerant towards me. •You (C3)
see, the jealousy that I feel for you is God's
own jealousy: I arranged for you to marry
Christ so that I might give you away as a (C3)
3 chaste virgin to this one husband. •But the (C2)
serpent, with his cunning, seduced Eve, and (C2)
I am afraid that in the same way your ideas
may get corrupted and turned away from sim-
4 ple devotion to Christ. •Because any new- (C2)
comer has only to proclaim a new Jesus, different from the one that we preached, or you
have only to receive a new spirit, different
from the one you have already received, or
a new gospel, different from the one you have
already accepted—and you welcome it with (C2)
5 open arms. •As far as I can tell, these arch-
6 apostles have nothing more than I have. •I
may not be a polished speechmaker, but as
for knowledge, that is a different matter;
surely we have made this plain, speaking on (C1)
every subject in front of all of you.

7 Or was I wrong, lowering myself so as to (C3)
lift you high, by preaching the gospel of God
8 to you and taking no fee for it? •I was robbing (C3)
other churches living on them so that I could (C3)
9 serve you. •When I was with you and ran out
of money, I was no burden to anyone; the (C3)
brothers who came from Macedonia provided me with everything I wanted. I was
very careful, and I always shall be, not to be
10 a burden to you in any way, •and by Christ's (C3)
truth in me, this cause of boasting will never
be taken from me in the regions of Achaia.
11 Would I do that if I did not love you? God (C3)
12 knows I do. •I intend to go on doing what I
am doing now—leaving no opportunity for
those people who are looking for an opportunity to claim equality with us in what they (C2)
13 boast of. •These people are counterfeit apos- (C2)
tles, they are dishonest workmen disguised
14 as apostles of Christ. •There is nothing unexpected about that; if Satan himself goes dis- (C2)
15 guised as an angel of light, •there is no need
to be surprised when his servants, too, disguise themselves as the servants of right- (C2)
eousness. They will come to the end that they
deserve.
16 As I said before, let no one take me for

150

a fool; but if you must, then treat me as a fool
and let me do a little boasting of my own.
17 What I am going to say now is not prompted
by the Lord, but said as if in a fit of folly, in
the certainty that I have something to boast
18 about. ·So many others have been boasting (C2)
of their worldly achievements, that I will
19 boast myself. ·You are all wise men and can
20 cheerfully tolerate fools, ·yes, even to tolerat-
ing somebody who makes slaves of you, (C2)
makes you feed him, imposes on you, orders (C2)
21 you about and slaps you in the face. ·I hope
you are ashamed of us for being weak with
you instead!

But if anyone wants some brazen speaking—I am still talking as a fool—then I can
be as brazen as any of them, and about the
22 same things. ·Hebrews, are they? So am I.
Israelites? So am I. Descendants of Abra-
23 ham? So am I. ·The servants of Christ? I
must be mad to say this, but so am I, and (C3)
more than they: more, because I have worked
harder, I have been sent to prison more often,
and whipped so many times more, often al-
24 most to death. ·Five times I had the thirty- (C2)
25 nine lashes from the Jews; ·three times I have (C2)
been beaten with sticks; once I was stoned; (C2)
three times I have been shipwrecked and
once adrift in the open sea for a night and a
26 day. ·Constantly traveling, I have been in (C4)
danger from rivers and in danger from brig- (C2)
ands, in danger from my own people and in (C2)
danger from pagans; in danger in the towns,
in danger in the open country, danger at sea (C2)
27 and danger from so-called brothers. ·I have
worked and labored, often without sleep; I (C3)
have been hungry and thirsty and often starving; I have been in the cold without clothes.
28 And, to leave out much more, there is my (C3)
daily preoccupation: my anxiety for all the
29 churches. ·When any man has had scruples, (C3)
I have had scruples with him; when any man (C3)
is made to fall, I am tortured.

30 If I am to boast, then let me boast of my
31 own feebleness. ·The God and Father of the
Lord Jesus—bless him for ever—knows that (C2)
32 I am not lying. ·When I was in Damascus, the
ethnarch of King Aretas put guards round the
33 city to catch me, ·and I had to be let down
over the wall in a hamper, through a window,
in order to escape.

Week 2 Day 5
Four C's Meditations
on 2 Corinthians 10:1-11:33

1.   Most Merciful Savior, in the Scripture
reading for today St. Paul describes his work
on behalf of the Corinthian Church as one of
combat. [70] It was a combat waged against
false apostles who were weakening, if not
destroying, the Church at Corinth. They were
accomplishing this by diluting and perverting
the true doctrine You had commissioned
Your genuine Apostles to teach in its entirety
and purity.

2.   Actually Paul's combat was a spiritual
one, waged ultimately not against the false
apostles, but against the invisible forces of evil

whom the false apostles, perhaps inadvertently, served. And there can be no doubt that these evil forces, headed by satan, ardently desired the total destruction of Your Mystical Body, the Church. *(For more about the nature of this spiritual combat see Ephesians 6:10-17.)*

3.   This fact, Lord, serves to remind us that it is not only the sins of the world and the flesh that are our enemies, but also satan himself, together with his fellow fallen angels. For those striving to live in Your intimate friendship, it would be foolhardy to suppose satan and his legions were not at the same time seeking to frustrate their efforts. Consequently, it is alway necessary to cling to You in prayer and to accept as true no religious doctrine except that taught by Your Holy Catholic Church. Nor should the faithful neglect to receive the sacraments of Penance and the Eucharist frequently, nor fail to seek the powerful intercession of Your saints, especially of Our Lady and St. Michael the Archangel.

4. We noted also, Jesus, that St. Paul expected from the Christians in Corinth complete obedience to his apostolic authority.[71] At first sight this might seem like a contradiction to Your own teaching to the Apostles when You said:

5. "You know that among the pagans the rulers lord it over them, and the great men make their authority felt. This is not to happen among you. No; anyone who wants to be great among you must be your servant, and anyone who wants to be first among you must be your slave, just as the Son of Man came not to be served but to serve, and to give his life as a ransom for many."[72]

6. Those who govern us in the Church should do so as ones who serve us with what is necessary for our salvation, e.g., the sacraments and Catholic doctrine. And we who are under their authority owe them our loving obedience. In this way the Church functions and grows smoothly and peacefully.

7. Jesus, Mary and Joseph, help us to be more obedient to those holding legitimate authority in the Church, knowing that by doing so the whole Church benefits. Particularly, help us to obey at all times the Pope and the bishops who teach and govern with him as their head. Moreover, may parents wisely and charitably govern their children, and constantly remind them that one day they will have to render an accounting to God for their children's conduct. In addition, help children to obey their parents at all times.

8. In chapter 11, Jesus, St. Paul warns the Corinthians not to receive any doctrine except what he had given them. To do otherwise, he warned, would be to accept a new or different gospel and a new Jesus, a Jesus having no existence outside of the minds of the false teachers. [73]

9. Lord, Catholics should be very thankful that what You taught the Apostles has been safely handed down through the centuries by the Popes and the bishops in communion with them. With this in mind we should always reject any doctrine which does not reflect the teaching of the Church of Rome. To do otherwise would be to accept false teaching and contribute to the weakening of Your Church, to say nothing of the danger we would be placing our souls in. *(For a detailed presentation on the role of the Pope and bishops in doctrinal matters, read pp. 219-233 of "The Catholic Catechism.")*

10. Finally Lord, St. Paul makes an appeal to the Corinthians to be loyal to him and to the doctrine he received from You. He reminds them that he has suffered, as both Your servant and theirs, far more than any of the false apostles. [74]

11. Who can deny, Lord, St. Paul's exceptional charity for You and for others, which was often accompanied by so much suffering? We should imagine that even among the saints as a whole, few suffered as much as St. Paul. He certainly is Your beloved son in whom You are well pleased. Together with

Yourself he is a magnificent model of seed-charity for us to imitate. And surely we can rely on his help when we suffer from time to time for Your sake and for the sake of our fellow men. "Blessed be God in His angels and in His saints." Amen.

Try to read these Scripture passages and meditations in a reflective manner every day. The Holy spirit will reveal more insights to you each time you do so.

Please read and meditate on Chapter V, Paragraphs 1 to 18 in our "Prayers and Recommended Practices" book.

WEEK 2 DAY 6
2 Corinthians 12:1-13:13

1 **12** Must I go on boasting, though there is nothing to be gained by it? But I will move on to the visions and revelations I have 2 had from the Lord. ·I know a man in Christ who, fourteen years ago, was caught up— whether still in the body or out of the body, I do not know; God knows—right into the 3 third heaven.^a ·I do know, however, that this same person—whether in the body or out of 4 the body, I do not know; God knows—·was

caught up into paradise and heard things
which must not and cannot be put into human
5 language. •I will boast about a man like that,
but not about anything of my own except my
6 weaknesses. •If I should decide to boast, I
should not be made to look foolish, because (C2)
I should only be speaking the truth; but I am
not going to, in case anyone should begin to
think I am better than he can actually see and
hear me to be.

7   In view of the extraordinary nature of these
revelations, to stop me from getting too (C2)
proud I was given a thorn in the flesh, an
angel of Satan to beat me and stop me from
8 getting too proud! •About this thing, I have (C2)
pleaded with the Lord three times for it to
9 leave me, •but he has said, "My grace is
enough for you: my power is at its best in
weakness." So I shall be very happy to make
my weaknesses my special boast so that the
10 power of Christ may stay over me, •and that
is why I am quite content with my weak- (C2)
nesses, and with insults, hardships, persecutions, and the agonies I go through for (C3)
Christ's sake. For it is when I am weak that
I am strong.

11   I have been talking like a fool, but you
forced me to do it: you are the ones who
should have been commending me. Though
I am a nobody, there is not a thing these
arch-apostles have that I do not have as well.
12 You have seen done among you all the things
that mark the true apostle, unfailingly pro-
duced: the signs, the marvels, the miracles.
13 Is there anything of which you have had less
than the other churches have had, except that
I have not myself been a burden on you? For (C3)
14 this unfairness, please forgive me. •I am all
prepared now to come to you for the third
time, and I am not going to be a burden on (C3)
you: it is you I want, not your possessions.
Children are not expected to save up for their
15 parents, but parents for children. •I am per- (C3)

fectly willing to spend what I have, and to be expended, in the interests of your souls. Because I love you more, must I be loved the less? (C3)

16 All very well, you say: I personally put no pressure on you, but like the cunning fellow 17 that I am, I took you in by a trick. ·So we exploited you, did we, through one of the 18 men that I have sent to you? ·Well, Titus went at my urging, and I sent the brother that came with him. Can Titus have exploited you? You know that he and I have always been guided by the same spirit and trodden in the same tracks.

Paul's fears and anxieties

19 All this time you have been thinking that our defense is addressed to you, but it is before God that we, in Christ, are speaking; and it is all, my dear brothers, for your bene-20 fit. ·What I am afraid of is that when I come I may find you different from what I want you to be, and you may find that I am not as you would like me to be; and then there will be (C2) wrangling, jealousy, and tempers roused, intrigues and backbiting and gossip, obstina-21 cies and disorder. ·I am afraid that on my next (C3) visit, my God may make me ashamed on your (C2) account and I shall be grieving over all those

who sinned before and have still not repented of the impurities, fornication and debauchery (C2) they committed.

1 **13**This will be the third time I have come to you. *The evidence of three, or at least two, witnesses is necessary to sustain the* 2 *charge.ª* ·I gave warning when I was with you the second time and I give warning now, too, before I come, to those who sinned before (C2) and to any others, that when I come again, 3 I shall have no mercy. ·You want proof, you say, that it is Christ speaking in me: you have known him not as a weakling, but as a power 4 among you? ·Yes, but he was crucified through weakness, and still he lives now through the power of God. So then, we are weak, as he was, but we shall live with him, through the power of God, for your benefit.

5 Examine yourselves to make sure you are (C1) in the faith; test yourselves. Do you acknowledge that Jesus Christ is really in you? If not, 6 you have failed the test, ·but we, as I hope 7 you will come to see, have not failed it. ·We pray to God that you will do nothing wrong· (C2) not that we want to appear as the ones who have been successful—we would rather that 8 you did well even though we failed. ·We have no power to resist the truth; only to further 9 it. ·We are only too glad to be weak provided you are strong. What we ask in our prayers (C3) 10 is for you to be made perfect. ·That is why I am writing this from a distance, so that when I am with you I shall not need to be strict, with the authority which the Lord gave (C3) me for building up and not for destroying.

CONCLUSION

Recommendations. Greetings. Final good wishes

11 In the meantime, brothers, we wish you happiness; try to grow perfect; help one an- (C3) other. Be united; live in peace, and the God

of love and peace will be with you.

12 Greet one another with the holy kiss. All ^(C3)
the saints send you greetings.

13 The grace of the Lord Jesus Christ, the
love of God and the fellowship of the Holy
Spirit be with you all.

Week 2 Day 6
Four C's Meditations
on 2 Corinthians 12:1-13:13

1. Most Sacred Heart of Jesus, You assured
Your servant St. Paul with these words: "My
grace is enough for you: my power is at its
best in weakness."⁽⁷⁵⁾ In response Your
Apostle wrote: "So shall I be very happy to
make my weaknesses my special boast so that
the power of Christ may stay over me, and
that is why I am content with my weaknesses,
and with insults, hardships, persecutions, and
the agonies I go through for Christ's sake. For
it is when I am weak that I am strong."⁽⁷⁶⁾

2. These words, Divine Lord, reflect the
great love St. Paul had both for You and for
others. He was content with his weaknesses

and sufferings, because he was confident You were using them to attract many to Your Church.

3. And, of course, this was indeed the case. Through Paul's ministry, accompanied by physical weaknesses and many sufferings, it was obvious to those who accepted You that You were working through him.

4. They must have concluded something like this, "No man who is so weak could endure what he continually endures unless the Christ is with him as he claims. How could such a fragile person work such mighty wonders unless God is with him? Surely, then, this Christ whom he preaches is the Savior of the world as he maintains, and therefore our Savior as well." If this were not the case, why would St. Paul have said, "For it is when I am weak that I am strong?" Meaning that when he was weak, You and Your saving power were working through him with transparent clarity.

5. St. Paul also notes, Lord, that it was through Your own weakness on the Cross that the saving power of God became operative in the world.

6. "You want proof, you say, that it is Christ speaking in me: you have known him not as a weakling, but as a power among you? Yes, but he was crucified through weakness, and still he lives now through the power of God. So then, we are weak, as he was, but we shall live with him, through the power of God, for your benefit."[77]

7. Jesus, Our Lord and Savior, how many moral weaknesses we have! May we always turn to You in humility for the comfort of Your healing graces. We are confident that through them we will be strengthened and, therefore, become more and more God-centered. Lord, may this strengthening be a sign for others of Your almighty power so that they may be brought ever closer to You, enjoying the consolations of Your perfect charity.

8. Also, Lord, how many physical weaknesses we have! May they also be used by You to further the growth of Your Kingdom on earth.

9. Jesus, Savior of the world, in today's meditation St. Paul writes that he prayed for the perfection of the Christians at Corinth. Additionally, he urged the Corinthians to their face, so to speak, to consciously strive to be perfect; thus reflecting Your own teaching when You said, "You must be perfect just as your heavenly Father is perfect."[78] To be perfect in this life is to be as holy as possible.

This involves a constant striving. And the perfection we will gain will always fall short of the perfection that will be ours in Heaven. In essence, to strive for perfection means we should be striving to use seed-charity constantly in our thoughts, words and deeds. In doing so we shall be increasingly like the Father, and like You, Who are the most perfect image of the Father.

10. On the negative side, in order to become more perfect, Lord, we must be detached from all that would prevent the full use of seed-charity. Consequently, we must desire to be detached from not only mortal sins but from venial sins as well. And we must continually ask for supernatural strength to accomplish these goals.

11. Most merciful Jesus, help us to examine our consciences carefully every day, and give us the grace to remove whatever in them is displeasing to You. Help us to make them pure and sinless. Especially, fill us with that most excellent gift of charity, the queen of all virtues.

12. Finally, we noted in our meditation, Jesus, that St. Paul was concerned that he might encounter a lack of seed-charity when he revisited his spiritual children in Corinth. He was afraid there might be, "wrangling, jealousy, and tempers roused, intrigues and back-biting and gossip, obstinacies and disorder."[79] Moreover, he was afraid that he might find sexual impurity, fornication and debauchery. [80]

163

13. Sin, Lord, is self-centered and divisive. Sin is a reflection of our selfishness which serves to bring disorder and chaos into communities such as families, parishes, neighborhoods and nations. Mortal sin is particularly atrocious, because it cuts us off from Your charity and friendship. And it is Your charity and friendship which we need in order to become less and less sinful, so that peace, joy and happiness can reign in us as individuals, and in communities, large and small.

14. Lord, as each one of us works to develop a pure conscience by becoming less self-centered and more God-centered through the graces of constancy, confidence, and seed-charity, we contribute to peace and stability and to the happiness of families, parishes, neighborhoods and nations.

15. Lord, by the power of Your Holy Spirit, the Spirit of charity, inspire us to always be aware of the hideousness of sin, so that we will work all the harder to overcome it through Your grace. Amen.

Try to re-read and re-meditate on these Scripture passages and reflections at least one more time today.

Please read and meditate on Chapter V, Paragraphs 19 to 28 in our "Prayers and Recommended Practices" book.

Galatians

THE LETTER OF PAUL
TO THE CHURCH
IN GALATIA

Address

1 2 **1** From Paul to the churches of Galatia, and from all the brothers who are here with me, an apostle who does not owe his authority to men or his appointment to any human being but who has been appointed by Jesus Christ and by God the Father who (C3) 3 raised Jesus from the dead. •We wish you the grace and peace of God our Father and of the 4 Lord Jesus Christ, •who in order to rescue us from this present wicked world sacrificed (C3) himself for our sins, in accordance with the (C2) 5 will of God our Father, •to whom be glory (C3) for ever and ever. Amen.

A warning

6   I am astonished at the promptness with

165

which you have turned away from the one (C2)
who called you and have decided to follow
7 a different version of the Good News. •Not
that there can be more than one Good News;
it is merely that some troublemakers among (C2)
you want to change the Good News of
8 Christ; •and let me warn you that if anyone
preaches a version of the Good News differ- (C2)
ent from the one we have already preached
to you, whether it be ourselves or an angel
9 from heaven, he is to be condemned. •I am
only repeating what we told you before: if
anyone preaches a version of the Good News (C2)
different from the one you have already
10 heard, he is to be condemned. •So now whom
am I trying to please—man, or God? Would
you say it is men's approval I am looking (C2)
for?*a* If I still wanted that, I should not be (C3)
what I am—a servant of Christ.

I. PAUL'S APOLOGIA

God's call

11 The fact is, brothers, and I want you to
realize this, the Good News I preached is not
12 a human message •that I was given by men,
it is something I learned only through a reve-
13 lation of Jesus Christ. •You must have heard
of my career as a practicing Jew, how merci- (C2)
less I was in persecuting the Church of God,
14 how much damage I did to it, •how I stood
out among other Jews of my generation, and
how enthusiastic I was for the traditions of
my ancestors.
15 Then God, who had specially *chosen* me
while I was *still in my mother's womb,b* called
16 me through his grace and chose •to reveal his
Son in me, so that I might preach the Good (C3)
News about him to the pagans. I did not stop
17 to discuss this with any human being, •nor did
I go up to Jerusalem to see those who were
already apostles before me, but I went off to

Arabia*c* at once and later went straight back
18 from there to Damascus. ·Even when after
three years I went up to Jerusalem to visit
Cephas and stayed with him for fifteen days,
19 I did not see any of the other apostles; I only
20 saw James, the brother of the Lord, ·and I
swear before God that what I have just writ-
21 ten is the literal truth. ·After that I went to
22 Syria and Cilicia, ·and was still not known by
sight to the churches of Christ in Judaea,
23 who had heard nothing except that their one-
time persecutor was now preaching the faith (c 3)
24 he had previously tried to destroy; ·and they (c2)
gave glory to God for me.

The meeting at Jerusalem

1 **2** It was not till fourteen years had passed
that I went up to Jerusalem again. I went
2 with Barnabas and took Titus with me. ·I
went there as the result of a revelation, and
privately I laid before the leading men the
Good News as I proclaim it among the pagans; I did so for fear the course I was adopt-
ing or had already adopted would not be al-
3 lowed. ·And what happened? Even though
Titus who had come with me is a Greek, he
4 was not obliged to be circumcised. ·The
question came up only because some who do
not really belong to the brotherhood have

167

furtively crept in to spy on the liberty we (C2)
enjoy in Christ Jesus, and want to reduce us
5 all to slavery. ·I was so determined to safe- (C3)
guard for you the true meaning of the Good
News, that I refused even out of deference (C3)

6 to yield to such people for one moment. ·As
a result, these people who are acknowledged
leaders—not that their importance matters to
me, since God has no favorites—these leaders, as I say, had nothing to add to the Good
7 News as I preach it. ·On the contrary, they
recognized that I had been commissioned to
preach the Good News to the uncircumcised
just as Peter had been commissioned to
8 preach it to the circumcised. ·The same person whose action had made Peter the apostle
of the circumcised had given me a similar
9 mission to the pagans. ·So, James, Cephas
and John, these leaders, these pillars, shook
hands with Barnabas and me as a sign of
partnership: we were to go to the pagans and
10 they to the circumcised.*a* ·The only thing they
insisted on was that we should remember to
help the poor, as indeed I was anxious to do.

Peter and Paul at Antioch

11 When Cephas came to Antioch, however, (C3)
I opposed him to his face, since he was mani- (C2)

12 festly in the wrong. ·His custom had been to (C3)
eat with the pagans,*b* but after certain friends
of James arrived he stopped doing this and
kept away from them altogether for fear of (C2)
13 the group that insisted on circumcision. ·The (C2)
other Jews joined him in this pretense, and
even Barnabas felt himself obliged to copy
their behavior. (C2)
14 When I saw they were not respecting the
true meaning of the Good News, I said to (C2)
Cephas in front of everyone, "In spite of being a Jew, you live like the pagans and not
like the Jews, so you have no right to make
the pagans copy Jewish ways."

168

15 "Though we were born Jews and not (C2)
16 pagan sinners, •we acknowledge that what
makes a man righteous is not obedience to (C1)
the Law, but faith in Jesus Christ. We had to
become believers in Christ Jesus no less than
you had, and now we hold that faith in Christ (C1)
rather than fidelity to the Law is what justifies
us, and that *no one can be justified*ᶜ by keep-
17 ing the Law. •Now if we were to admit that
the result of looking to Christ to justify us
is to make us sinners like the rest, it would (C2)
follow that Christ had induced us to sin,
18 which would be absurd. •If I were to return
to a position I had already abandoned, I
should be admitting I had done something
19 wrong. •In other words, through the Law I (C3)
am dead to the Law, so that now I can live
for God. I have been crucified with Christ,
20 and I live now not with my own life but with (C3)
the life of Christ who lives in me. The life
I now live in this body I live in faith: faith in
the Son of God who loved me and who sacri- (C1)
21 ficed himself for my sake. •I cannot bring
myself to give up God's gift: if the Law can
justify us, there is no point in the death of
Christ."

Week 2 Day 7
Four C's Meditations
on Galatians 1:1-2:21

1. Most Sacred Heart of Jesus, today's Scripture reading is taken from St. Paul's letter to the Church in Galatia (now in modern Turkey). Moreover, when we compare St. Paul's description of the Christians in Galatia to those in Corinth, we note that members of both communities were disloyal to the Gospel preached to them by St. Paul. *(Be sure to read the introductory remarks about this letter found in Paragraphs 67-72 of the introduction to this book.)*

2. In the Church in Galatia the culprits primarily responsible for the disloyalty were certain Jewish "converts." These insisted that Gentile or non-Jewish Christians observe the Old Testament Law of Moses with its regulations governing sacrifices and ritual purity. Furthermore, as a sign of commitment to the Old Testament Law, these "Judaizers" maintained that all male Christians must be circumcised. Consequently, they were implying that salvation did not come entirely from Christ, but also from observing the Old Testament Law of Moses.

3. As You know, Divine King, St. Paul chided the Galatian Christians for turning from the true Gospel and for accepting the false gospel of the Judaizers.[81] He stressed the fact that salvation or justification comes only from You, and not from the Old Testament legal prescriptions which were

incapable of justifying anyone.[82] Therefore, he taught that the Mosaic ritual precepts were not binding on Christians, whether they were originally Jewish or Gentile.

4. St. Paul adds, Lord, that the Judaizers were in effect trying to lead the Galatians into slavery, i.e., a slavery to the Mosaic Law. Whereas, only the true Gospel, previously received by the Galatians, was capable of liberating them from sin and death. Through the acceptance of the Gospel, by means of faith and charity, they were given the grace to become saints and become heirs of everlasting life in Your heavenly Kingdom.

5. Next, Jesus, our attention dwelt on the only recorded instance of moral weakness associated with St. Peter since he had become Your Vicar and the Prince of the Apostles.

6. As Your Vicar he came to the realization that You wanted neither the Jewish nor the Gentile Christians to be burdened by the Law of Moses.[83] But subsequently there was a brief period when he betrayed his conscience in this matter.[84]

7. Whereas, he was previously accustomed, and correctly so, to eating with pagan (Gentile) Christians, he now refused to do so. This was due to the presence of the Judaizers who objected to the practice since the Old Testament Law forbade Jews, such as St. Peter, to eat with Gentiles. Not only did St. Peter, now a Jewish Christian, act against his conscience in this matter but he also scandalized the Gentile Christians. Furthermore, his conduct was particularly scandalous since as the head of the Church he should have set an example of holy and courageous conduct for everyone.

8. It is not surprising then, Lord, knowing the temperment of St. Paul, that he scolded St. Peter to his face for his cowardly behavior.

9. Unfortunately, Most Sacred Heart of Jesus, at times we are more like St. Peter than St. Paul. St. Paul was a man with great natural courage, possessing an iron will. Moreover, Your supernatural grace served to strengthen his courage and resolve to serve the cause of revealed truth. St. Peter, on the other hand, as most of us will recall, was by nature somewhat impulsive and lacking in great courage.

10. Yet Your grace marvelously transformed him, giving him a boldness he previously lacked. Nonetheless, the presence of the Judaizers at Antioch triggered a momentary relapse into his old weakness.[85]

11. Lord, often we have been ashamed to

defend the Faith You have given Your Church. We have sometimes been afraid others might think we are foolish, stupid or naive. And we have often rationalized our lack of pure consciences in this regard by saying we don't want to offend anyone or hurt their feelings. Jesus, You, Your teaching and Your Church are challenged and attacked every day. And You have called us to be Your defenders and to uphold Your doctrine and Your Church. Yet time and again we fail to do so.

12. Lord, help us always to recall the example of St. Paul and that of the many other martyrs and defenders of the Faith. Throughout the ages they acted habitually with the faith, trust and seed-charity You had given them. Inspire us to shy away from cowardice, especially when it comes to matters of Your Faith and Your Church, knowing that You will be pleased because of our loyalty.

13. As You once said, "Do not be afraid of those who kill the body but cannot kill the soul; fear him rather who can destroy both

body and soul in hell."[86] Again, You said, "So if anyone declares himself for me in the presence of men, I will declare myself for him in the presence of my Father in heaven. But the one who disowns me in the presence of men, I will disown in the presence of my Father in heaven."[87]

14. Lord, may we always confess You, Your doctrine and Your Church before men. Give us enough faith, trust and seed-charity ·so that we will be both afraid and ashamed not to do so.

15. Finally, Lord, St. Paul points out to the Gentile Christians the futility of the Mosaic Law to give salvation. He writes that as a Christian he was dead to the demands of the Law. He was now crucified with You. That is, he was dead to the power of sin and death and alive to Your marvelous life which dwelt in him, giving him faith, hope, and seed-charity. And these nurtured him in sanctity.[88]

16. Jesus, may we always be dead to sin and alive to the life-giving virtues of confidence (faith, hope) and seed-charity which You merited for us by Your Cross and Passion. Amen.

The more you re-read these Scriptures and meditations, the more you will get out of them.

Please read and meditate in our "Prayers and Recommended Practices" book on Chapter VI, Paragraphs 1 to 4; and on Chapter VII containing the Litany of the Patrons of The Apostolate.

II. DOCTRINAL MATTERS

Justification by faith

1 **3** Are you people in Galatia mad? Has someone put a spell on you, in spite of the plain explanation you have had of the cruci-
2 fixion of Jesus Christ? ·Let me ask you one question: was it because you practiced the Law that you received the Spirit, or because (C1)
3 you believed what was preached to you? ·Are you foolish enough to end in outward observ- (C2)
4 ances what you began in the Spirit? ·Have all the favors you received been wasted? And if this were so, they would most certainly
5 have been wasted. ·Does God give you the Spirit so freely and work miracles among you because you practice the Law, or be-cause you believed what was preached to (C1) you?

6 Take Abraham for example: *he put his* (C1) *faith in God, and this faith was considered as*
7 *justifying him.ᵃ* ·Don't you see that it is those (C1) who rely on faith who are the sons of
8 Abraham? ·Scripture foresaw that God was going to use faith to justify the pagans, and proclaimed the Good News long ago when

Abraham was told: *In you all the pagans will*
9 *be blessed.*[b] •Those therefore who rely on (C1)
faith receive the same blessing as Abraham, (C1)
the man of faith.

The curse brought by the Law

10   On the other hand, those who rely on the
keeping of the Law are under a curse, since
scripture says: *Cursed by everyone who does* (C1)
not persevere in observing everything pre-
11 *scribed in the book of the Law.*[c] •The Law will
not justify anyone in the sight of God, because we are told: *the righteous man finds life* (C1)
12 *through faith.*[d] •The Law is not even based
on faith, since we are told: *The man who*
practices these precepts finds life through
13 *practicing them.*[e] •Christ redeemed us from
the curse of the Law by being cursed for our
sake, since scripture says: *Cursed be everyone*
14 *who is hanged on a tree.*[f] •This was done so
that in Christ Jesus the blessing of Abraham might include the pagans, and so that
through faith we might receive the promised (C1)
Spirit.

The Law did not cancel the promise

15   Compare this, brothers, with what happens
in ordinary life. If a will has been drawn up
in due form, no one is allowed to disregard
16 it or add to it. •Now the promises were addressed to Abraham *and to his descendants*
—notice, in passing, that scripture does not
use a plural word as if there were several
descendants, it uses the singular: to his pos-
17 terity, which is Christ. •But my point is this:
once God had expressed his will in due form,
no law that came four hundred and thirty
years later could cancel that and make the
18 promise meaningless. •If you inherit something as a legal right, it does not come to you
as the result of a promise, and it was precisely
in the form of a promise that God made his
gift to Abraham.

The purpose of the Law

19 What then was the purpose of adding the Law? This was done to specify crimes, until the posterity came to whom the promise was addressed. The Law was promulgated by an-
20 gels,*g* assisted by an intermediary. ·Now there can only be an intermediary between
21 two parties, yet God is one. ·Does this mean that there is opposition between the Law and the promises of God? Of course not. We could have been justified by the Law if the Law we were given had been capable of giv-
22 ing life, ·but it is not: scripture makes no exceptions when it says that sin is master everywhere. In this way the promise can only be given through faith in Jesus Christ (CI) and can only be given to those who have (CI) this faith.

The coming of faith

23 Before faith came, we were allowed no (CI) freedom by the Law; we were being looked
24 after till faith was revealed. ·The Law was to be our guardian until the Christ came and we (CI)
25 could be justified by faith. ·Now that that time has come we are no longer under that guard-
26 ian, ·and you are, all of you, sons of God (CI)
27 through faith in Christ Jesus. ·All baptized in Christ, you have all clothed yourselves in
28 Christ, ·and there are no more distinctions between Jew and Greek, slave and free, male and female, but all of you are one in Christ
29 Jesus. ·Merely by belonging to Christ you are the posterity of Abraham, the heirs he was promised.

Sons of God

1 **4** Let me put this another way: an heir, even if he has actually inherited everything, is no different from a slave for as long as he
2 remains a child. ·He is under the control of guardians and administrators until he

3 reaches the age fixed by his father. ·Now before we came of age we were as good as slaves to the elemental principles of this 4 world,*ᵃ* ·but when the appointed time came, God sent his Son, born of a woman, born a 5 subject of the Law, ·to redeem the subjects of the Law and to enable us to be adopted 6 as sons. ·The proof that you are sons is that God has sent the Spirit of his Son into our hearts: the Spirit that cries, "Abba, Father," 7 and it is this that makes you a son, you are not a slave any more; and if God has made you son, then he has made you heir.

8 Once you were ignorant of God, and en- (C2) slaved to "gods" who are not really gods at 9 all; ·but now that you have come to acknowl- edge God—or rather, now that God has ac- knowledged you—how can you want to go back to elemental things like these, that can do nothing and give nothing, and be (C2) 10 their slaves? ·You and your special days 11 and months and seasons and years! ·You make me feel I have wasted my time with you.

A personal appeal

12 Brothers, all I ask is that you should copy me as I copied you. You have never treated 13 me in an unfriendly way before; ·even at the

beginning, when that illness gave me the op- (C3)
portunity to preach the Good News to you,
14 you never showed the least sign of being (C2)
revolted or disgusted by my disease that was
such a trial to you; instead you welcomed me (C3)
as an angel of God, as if I were Christ Jesus
15 himself. ·What has become of this enthusiasm you had? I swear that you would
even have gone so far as to pluck out your
16 eyes and give them to me. ·Is it telling you (C3)
17 the truth that has made me your enemy? ·The (C2)
blame lies in the way they have tried to win
you over: by separating you from me, they
18 want to win you over to themselves. ·It is (C2)
always a good thing to win people over—and
I do not have to be there with you—but it
19 must be for a good purpose, ·my children! I ·
must go through the pain of giving birth to
you all over again, until Christ is formed in (C3)
20 you. ·I wish I were with you now so that I
could know exactly what to say; as it is, I have
no idea what to do for the best.

The two covenants: Hagar and Sarah

21   You want to be subject to the Law? Then
22 listen to what the Law says. ·It says, if you
remember, that Abraham had two sons, one
by the slave-girl, and one by his free-born
23 wife. ·The child of the slave-girl was born in
the ordinary way; the child of the free woman
24 was born as the result of a promise. ·This can
be regarded as an allegory: the women stand
for the two covenants. The first who comes
from Mount Sinai, and whose children are
25 slaves, is Hagar—·since Sinai is in Arabia
—and she corresponds to the present Jerusa-
26 lem that is a slave like her children. ·The
Jerusalem above, however, is free and is our
27 mother, ·since scripture says: *Shout for joy,*
you barren women who bore no children!
Break into shouts of joy and gladness, you
who were never in labor. For there are more

sons of the forsaken one than sons of the wed-
28 *ded wife.*[b] •Now you, my brothers, like Isaac,
29 are children of the promise, •and as at that
time the child born in the ordinary way persecuted the child born in the Spirit's way, so
30 also now. •Does not scripture say: *Drive*
away that slave-girl and her son; this slave-
girl's son is not to share the inheritance with
31 *the son*[c] of the free woman? •So, my brothers,
we are the children, not of the slave-girl, but
of the free-born wife.

Week 3 Day 1
Four C's Meditations
on Galatians 3:1-4:31

1. In today's meditation, Most Merciful
Lord, we were impressed by St. Paul's
fatherly solicitude for the Galatians whom he
had nurtured in the Faith. He was obviously
upset and disappointed with them for having
later abandoned the path to salvation. But
like a true parent he continued to love them.
He still longed for their salvation and took
pains to explain to them why the way they
had chosen was wrong.

2. Most Sacred Heart of Jesus, enable all Christian parents to follow St. Paul's example. Give them also the virtues of perseverance and charity, and may they use them generously in the rearing of their sons and daughters. At times their children exasperate and disappoint them. They sometimes feel let down, believing all their sacrifices for their offspring have been in vain. Some, feeling sorry for themselves, go so far as to wish their children had never been born.

3. But Lord, parents must never despair. Assure them You are always ready to support them in their parental duties. Forgive them, when recognizing they have failed in their responsibilities, they sorrowfully turn to You, the Source of all grace and the Refuge of sinners.

4. Blessed Savior, in his selfless concern for his lapsed children in Galatia, St. Paul endeavored to show them why they were wrong to substitute the Old Testament Law for the Good News of salvation he had previously preached to them.

5.   In essence, as we noted in yesterday's meditation, the Law was incapable of saving or justifying anyone. It was only through faith in You, Who are the very center and Source of The New Testament, that salvation was possible.

6.   Actually, there was nothing evil about the Law, since it was given to Moses by God. But in its observance, divorced from faith in You, there was no gift of Your sanctifying grace, which alone enables us to share in Your divine life and experience salvation even while living on earth. The Galatians, then, had exchanged the gift of everlasting life, which comes from faith in You, for the works of the Old Testament Law.

7.   Unfortunately, Jesus, many Christians over the centuries have also misinterpreted St. Paul's teachings on the necessity of faith for salvation. They concluded that not only the works of the Old Testament Law but also good works, inspired by the Holy Spirit, have nothing to do with our salvation. Consequently, they held we are saved by faith alone.

8.   Help them to understand that while we appropriate Your free gift of salvation by or through faith (belief) in You and in Your revelation, it must be faith which is perfected by works of seed-charity. Thus we appropriate and enhance salvation daily by our exercise of faith and supernatural charity. If we had faith alone without seed-charity, we would not be in the state of grace. We would not be in Your friendship. We would not have

access to salvation. *(For more on the relationship of faith to charity see "The Catholic Catechism." p. 571.)*

9. St. James, in a famous passage, stresses the necessary connection between faith and good (charitable) works.

10. "Take the case, my brothers, of someone who has never done a single good act but claims that he has faith. Will that faith save him? If one of the brothers or one of the sisters is in need of clothes and has not enough food to live on, and one of you says to them, 'I wish you well; keep yourself warm and eat plenty', without giving them these bare necessities of life, then what good is that? Faith is like that: if good works do not go with it, it is quite dead."[89]

11. St. Paul, as well, emphasized the necessity of both faith and charitable good works for our continued salvation and sanctification. "If I have faith in all its fullness, to move mountains, but without love, then I am nothing at all. If I give away all that I possess, piece by piece, and if I even let them take my body to burn it, but am without love, it will do me no good whatever."[90]

12. Today, Lord, there are also those who believe somewhat like the Galatians and their judaizing teachers. They hold, at least implicitly, that salvation somehow is entirely due to human good works. Thus they are foolishly saying that through their good works they are the real source of their own salvation. But as You told us, Jesus, "Without me you can do nothing."[91] This means that

without Your grace we cannot reach Heaven. We must, of course do our part. Through constant faith and charitable good works we must strive to acquire and retain Your gift of salvation, and through our efforts we must labor to grow in holiness. However, it is finally by Your grace that we are saved.

13.   Moreover, Lord, help us to realize that the performance of good works alone can never bring us salvation, nor can faith in You apart from good works performed with charity. Both together lead us not only to salvation, but to an earthly life of peaceful union with You as well. Amen.

May you, through the power of the Holy Spirit experience this gift of God's peace by slowly re-reading and re-meditating on the Scripture reading for today.

Please read and meditate on Chapter VIII, Paragraphs 1 to 16; Chapter IX, Paragraphs 1 to 27 in our "Prayers and Recommended Practices" book.

III. EXHORTATION

Christian liberty

1 **5** When Christ freed us, he meant us to remain free. Stand firm, therefore, and do (C4)
2 not submit again to the yoke of slavery. ·It (C2) is I, Paul, who tell you this: if you allow yourselves to be circumcised, Christ will be
3 of no benefit to you at all. ·With all solemnity I repeat my warning: Everyone who accepts circumcision is obliged to keep the whole
4 Law. ·But if you do look to the Law to make (C2) you justified, then you have separated yourselves from Christ, and have fallen from
5 grace. ·Christians are told by the Spirit to (C1) look to faith for those rewards that righteous-
6 ness hopes for, ·since in Christ Jesus whether you are circumcised or not makes no difference—what matters is faith that expresses (C1) itself in love.

7   You began your race well: who made you (C3)
8 less anxious to obey the truth? ·You were not
9 prompted by him who called you! ·The yeast seems to be spreading through the whole

10 batch of you. •I feel sure that, united in the Lord, you will agree with me, and anybody who troubles you in future will be con- (c2)
11 demned, no matter who he is. •As for me, my brothers, if I still preach circumcision,*a* why am I still persecuted? If I did that now, would (c2)
12 there be any scandal of the cross? •Tell those who are disturbing you I would like to see the knife slip.

Liberty and charity

13 My brothers, you were called, as you know, to liberty; but be careful, or this liberty will provide an opening for self-indulgence. (c2) Serve one another, rather, in works of love,
14 since the whole of the Law is summarized in (c3) a single command: *Love your neighbor as* (c3)
15 *yourself.*b •If you go snapping at each other (c2) and tearing each other to pieces, you had better watch or you will destroy the whole (c2) community.
16 Let me put it like this: if you are guided by the Spirit you will be in no danger of
17 yielding to self-indulgence, •since self-indul- (c2) gence is the opposite of the Spirit, the Spirit is totally against such a thing, and it is pre- cisely because the two are so opposed that you do not always carry out your good inten- (c2)
18 tions. •If you are led by the Spirit, no law can
19 touch you. •When self-indulgence is at work (c2) the results are obvious: fornication, gross (c2)
20 indecency and sexual irresponsibility; •idola- (c2) try and sorcery; feuds and wrangling, jeal- ousy, bad temper and quarrels; disagree-
21 ments, factions, •envy; drunkenness, orgies and similar things. I warn you now, as I (c2) warned you before: those who behave like this will not inherit the kingdom of God.
22 What the Spirit brings is very different: love, joy, peace, patience, kindness, goodness, (c3)
23 trustfulness, •gentleness and self-control. There can be no law against things like that,

24 of course. ·You cannot belong to Christ
Jesus unless you crucify all self-indulgent (C3)
passions and desires.

25   Since the Spirit is our life, let us be di- (C2)
26 rected by the Spirit. ·We must stop being
conceited, provocative and envious.   (C2)

On kindness and perseverance

1 **6**Brothers, if one of you misbehaves, the (C2)
more spiritual of you who set him right
should do so in a spirit of gentleness, not (C3)
forgetting that you may be tempted your-
2 selves. ·You should carry each other's trou- (C3)
3 bles and fulfill the law of Christ. ·It is
the people who are not important who of- (C2)
ten make the mistake of thinking that they
4 are. ·Let each of you examine his own conduct; if you find anything to boast about, it
will at least be something of your own,
not just something better than your neigh-
5 bour has. ·Everyone has his own burden to (C2)
carry.

6   People under instruction should always (C3)
contribute something to the support of the
man who is instructing them.

7   Don't delude yourself into thinking God (C2)
can be cheated: where a man sows, there he
8 reaps: ·if he sows in the field of self-indul- (C2)
gence he will get a harvest of corruption out
of it; if he sows in the field of the Spirit (C3)
he will get from it a harvest of eternal life.
9 We must never get tired of doing good be- (C3)
cause if we don't give up the struggle we
shall get our harvest at the proper time.
10 While we have the chance, we must do good (C3)
to all, and especially to our brothers in the
faith.

Epilogue

11   Take good note of what I am adding in my
12 own handwriting and in large letters. ·It is (C2)
only self-interest that makes them want to
force circumcision on you—they want to es- (C2)

cape persecution for the cross of Christ—

13 they accept circumcision but do not keep the ^(C2)
Law themselves; they only want you to be
circumcised so that they can boast of the fact.

14 As for me, the only thing I can boast about
is the cross of our Lord Jesus Christ, through
whom the world is crucified to me, and I to ^(C3)

15 the world. •It does not matter if a person is
circumcised or not; what matters is for him

16 to become an altogether new creature. •Peace
and mercy to all who follow this rule, who
form the Israel of God.

17   I want no more trouble from anybody after
this; the marks on my body are those of Jesus.

18 The grace of our Lord Jesus Christ be with ^(C3)
your spirit, my brothers. Amen.

**Week 3 Day 2
Four C's Meditations
on Galatians 5:1-6:18**

1.   Most Sacred Heart of Jesus, we found in
today's Scripture selection the ideas of both
slavery and freedom. But these were
presented in a religious rather than in a
political or economic sense. By slavery, St.
Paul meant bondage to the powers of sin and
death. It was these that enslaved the human
race when our first parents disobeyed You
and fell from Your favor.

2. By freedom, St. Paul meant freedom from sin and death. He also meant freedom to become holy. That is, freedom to love You and the Father and the Holy Spirit above all else, and freedom to love our neighbor as ourselves. Furthermore, he meant freedom to enjoy an everlasting happiness which You gained for us by Your selfless acts of love. Lord, when the Galatian Christians were still pagans they were slaves to the powers of sin and death. However, their later acceptance of the Good News of salvation, through the preaching of St. Paul, led them to the waters of Baptism. And in this sacrament they experienced the supernatural fruits of Your victory over sin and death. Furthermore, by the exercise of seed-charity, which they received in Baptism, they increasingly resembled Your perfect holiness and experienced inner peace and happiness.

3. Nevertheless, Most Holy Savior, the Judaizers induced many of the Galatians to embrace the Law of Moses, which we previously noted could not save or justify them. Thus, by vainly seeking salvation through the Mosaic Law they were once more subject to the powers of sin and death.

4. Divine Lord, teach us to confide in You alone as Savior. It is You alone Who can free us from our slavery to the forces of sin and death. Therefore, grant that we may accept no other religious doctrine, no matter how noble or true it may appear, than that which You bestowed on Your Church, through Your Apostles, for our salvation. And may

189

parents always take special pains to see that their children accept only the true Faith. *(See "The Catholic Catechism," pp. 234-236 about the necessity of the true Faith for salvation.)*

5. We noted also with interest, Lord, that in today's meditation St. Paul reinforced the teaching mentioned yesterday that charity, as well as faith, is necessary for our salvation.

6. "But if you do look to the Law to make you justified, then you have separated yourselves from Christ, and have fallen from grace. Christians are told by the Spirit to look to faith for those rewards that righteousness hopes for, since in Christ Jesus whether you are circumcised or not makes no difference — what matters is faith that expresses itself in love."[92]

7. Today, Lord, we observed that St. Paul made several references to self-indulgence which, he says, is opposed to the Holy Spirit. Moreover, he asserted that if we are guided by the Holy Spirit, self-indulgence will have no hold on us.

8.   Self-indulgence is an expression of pride, the root of all sins, which is actually self-centeredness. St. Paul listed several types of self-indulgence such as jealousy, quarreling, drunkeness and sexual perversity. He also maintained, Lord, that those who behave in this manner cannot inherit Your heavenly Kingdom.[93]

9.   Lord, when we give in to self-indulgence, we regard our selfish wills as more important than Your will. But this attitude is foolish, since it defiles our consciences and bars the entrance of Your Holy Spirit into our hearts where He longs to dwell as in a temple.[94] He, as St. Paul said, is opposed to self-indulgence because by His love he guides us away from sin into the way of Truth which leads to everlasting life. And You, Lord, as You have told us Yourself, are Truth itself.[95]

10.   When we are in the way of Truth through the Spirit's gift of seed-charity, we become God-centered, not self-centered. And our thoughts, words and deeds become God-centered. As a consequence we find real happiness as opposed to that unhappiness which is the fruit of self-indulgence.

11.   As St. Paul states, the Holy Spirit, by means of seed-charity, brings to the God-centered soul fruit that is quite different from the bitter fruit of self-indulgence. This spiritual fruit he describes as "love, joy, peace, patience, kindness, goodness, trustfulness, gentleness, and self-control."[96]

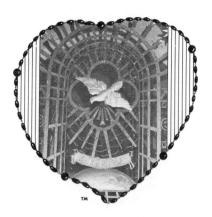

12. Jesus, though the path of self-indulgence is easy to follow, we know by faith, reason and experience that it can lead only to unhappiness. And we know by faith that it can ultimately lead us only to hell. By the power of Your Holy Spirit, cleanse our hearts of all self-indulgence and inspire us to perform acts of God-centered seed-charity which lead us to happiness and to Heaven. And we pray for all self-indulgent people that they will see the error of their ways and make their own the path of eternal life and joy.

13. Finally, heavenly King, our attention focused on St. Paul's desire for the Galatians to become altogether new creatures.[97] And elsewhere, he wrote, "And for anyone who is in Christ, there is a new creation; the old creation has gone, and now the new one is here."[98]

14. The old creation is that human nature subject to death and prone to sin with which we were conceived and born. The new creation is that which we received when we were baptised. At that time we had added to our nature sanctifying grace and various supernatural virtues and gifts, including confidence (faith and hope) and seed-charity. These enable us to share in Your divine life. In effect we became supernatural or divinized beings, whose destiny is the Beatific Vision of God and life everlasting. *(For more on the Beatific Vision, see "The Catholic Catechism," pp. 260-263.)*

15. If we use our supernatural gifts of faith, hope and seed-charity, Lord, we "new creatures" become increasingly like You in holiness, goodness and godliness. And the more like You we become, the more we are able to sacrifice ourselves effectively for You and for others. We will also find true happiness, and "that peace of God which is so much greater than we can understand."[99]

16. Lord, help us always to appreciate the magnificent gift of supernatural life which You gave us at Baptism. Moreover, help us to nourish it through fervent prayer and the devout reception of the sacraments. Amen.

Try to read these Scripture passages and meditations several times a day in a reflective manner. Each time you do so, the Holy Spirit will give you more insights.

Please read and meditate in our "Prayers and Recommended Practices" book, on Chapter X, Paragraphs 1 to 10; and on the Constant Vigil of Prayer found in Chapter XI.

Ephesians

THE LETTER OF PAUL
TO THE CHURCH
AT EPHESUS

Address and greetings

1 ¹ From Paul, appointed by God to be an
apostle of Christ Jesus, to the saints who
2 are faithful to Christ Jesus: ·Grace and peace
to you from God our Father and from the
Lord Jesus Christ.

I. THE MYSTERY OF
SALVATION AND OF
THE CHURCH

God's plan of salvation

3 Blessed be God the Father of our Lord Jesus ⁽ᶜ ³⁾
Christ,

who has blessed us with all the spiritual blessings of heaven in Christ.

4 Before the world was made, he chose us,
chose us in Christ,
to be holy and spotless, and to live through (C3)
love in his presence, (C3)

5 determining that we should become his
adopted sons, through Jesus Christ
for his own kind purposes,

6 to make us praise the glory of his grace, (C3)
his free gift to us in the Beloved,

7 in whom, through his blood, we gain our freedom, the forgiveness of our sins.
Such is the richness of the grace

8 which he has showered on us
in all wisdom and insight.

9 He has let us know the mystery of his purpose,
the hidden plan he so kindly made in Christ
from the beginning

10 to act upon when the times had run their
course to the end:
that he would bring everything together under Christ, as head,
everything in the heavens and everything on
earth.

11 And it is in him that we were claimed as
God's own,
chosen from the beginning,
under the predetermined plan of the one who

guides all things
as he decides by his own will;

12 chosen to be,
for his greater glory,
the people who would put their hopes in (CI)
Christ before he came.

13 Now you too, in him,
have heard the message of the truth and the
good news of your salvation,
and have believed it; (CI)
and you too have been stamped with the seal
of the Holy Spirit of the Promise,

14 the pledge of our inheritance
which brings freedom for those whom God
· has taken for his own,
to make his glory praised.

The triumph and the supremacy of Christ

15 That will explain why I, having once heard
about your faith in the Lord Jesus, and the (CI)
love that you show towards all the saints, (C3)

16 have never failed to remember you in my

17 prayers and to thank God for you. ·May the (C3)
God of our Lord Jesus Christ, the Father of
glory, give you a spirit of wisdom and perception of what is revealed, to bring you to full

18 knowledge of him. ·May he enlighten the
eyes of your mind so that you can see what (CI)
hope his call holds for you, what rich glories

19 he has promised the saints will inherit ·and
how infinitely great is the power that he has
exercised for us believers. This you can tell (CI)

20 from the strength of his power ·at work in
Christ, when he used it to raise him from the
dead and to make him sit at his right hand,

21 in heaven, ·far above every Sovereignty, Authority, Power, or Domination,*a* or any other
name that can be named, not only in this age

22 but also in the age to come. ·*He has put all
things under his feet,*b and made him, as the
ruler of everything, the head of the Church;

23 which is his body, the fullness of him who
fills the whole creation.

2 And you were dead, through the crimes (C2)
and the sins •in which you used to live
when you were following the way of this
world, obeying the ruler who governs the air,[a] (C2)
the spirit who is at work in the rebellious.
3 We all were among them too in the past, (C2)
living sensual lives, ruled entirely by our own
physical desires and our own ideas; so that (C2)
by nature we were as much under God's an-
4 ger as the rest of the world. •But God loved
us with so much love that he was generous
5 with his mercy: •when we were dead through (C2)
our sins, he brought us to life with Christ—it
is through grace that you have been saved—
6 and raised us up with him and gave us a place
with him in heaven, in Christ Jesus.
7 This was to show for all ages to come,
through his goodness toward us in Christ
Jesus, how infinitely rich he is in grace.
8 Because it is by grace that you have been
saved, through faith; not by anything of your (C1)
9 own, but by a gift from God; •not by anything that you have done, so that nobody can
10 claim the credit. •We are God's work of art,
created in Christ Jesus to live the good life (C3)

197

as from the beginning he had meant us to live it.

Reconciliation of the Jews and the pagans with each other and with God

11 Do not forget, then, that there was a time when you who were pagans physically, termed the Uncircumcised by those who speak of themselves as the Circumcision by 12 reason of a physical operation, ·do not forget, I say, that you had no Christ and were excluded from membership of Israel, aliens with no part in the covenants with their Promise; you were immersed in this world, without 13 hope and without God. ·But now in Christ Jesus, you that used to be so far apart from (C2) us have been brought very close, by the 14 blood of Christ. ·For he is the peace between us, and has made the two into one and broken down the barrier which used to keep them apart, actually destroying in his own person 15 the hostility ·caused by the rules and decrees of the Law. This was to create one single New Man in himself out of the two of them 16 and by restoring peace ·through the cross, to unite them both in a single Body and reconcile them with God. In his own person he 17 killed the hostility. ·Later he came to bring (C2) the good news of peace, *peace to you who were far away and peace to those who were* 18 *near at hand.*[b] ·Through him, both of us have in the one Spirit our way to come to the Father.

19 So you are no longer aliens or foreign visitors: you are citizens like all the saints, and 20 part of God's household. ·You are part of a building that has the apostles and prophets[c] for its foundations, and Christ Jesus himself 21 for its main cornerstone. ·As every structure (C1) is aligned on him, all grow into one holy (C2) 22 temple in the Lord; ·and you too, in him, are (C3) being built into a house where God lives, in the Spirit.

Week 3 Day 3
Four C's Meditations
on Ephesians 1:1-2:22

1.   Most Sacred Heart of Jesus, we have just begun to read St. Paul's Letter to the Ephesians. In it, he speaks of the mystery of the Father's selection before the world was made of those who would become Christians, i.e., His adopted sons and daughters. Moreover, Lord, St. Paul says Christians were chosen in You "to be holy and spotless, and to live through love" in the Father's presence.[100] *(Be sure to read the introductory remarks on Ephesians found in paragraphs 73-75 of the introduction to this book.)*

2.   Lord, we are grateful that we were freely chosen to be Christians and adopted sons and daughters of the Father. And we are particularly grateful that You were willing to sacrifice and humble Yourself for us so that our election might be possible. At times it is hard to believe that, in spite of our sinfulness, the Father loves us so much that He chose us to be members of His family even while we live here on earth.

3.   Our heavenly Father loves us so much that He treats us, not simply as creatures, but as His own offspring and Your brothers and sisters. And if we are Your brothers and sisters, Lord, then Your Blessed Mother is truly our Mother as well. What awesome thoughts! And what great love You have for us in that You willingly suffered and died so that You might be the Instrument of our elevation to salvation and sanctity.

4.   Jesus, we pray to You and to Your Most Holy Mother that we may never lose our status as Your adopted brothers and sisters. May we remain holy and spotless, and always live in the unseen presence of the Father through faith and acts of seed-charity.

5.   Lord, St. Paul also teaches us in today's meditation that the Jews were chosen for the "greater glory"[101] of the Father, and that Gentile Christians, freed from the bondage of sin and death, were chosen to "make His glory praised."[102]

6.   At first sight such language seems to convey the idea that the Father loves only Himself, and that we Christians were chosen solely to satisfy His apparent conceit. But this cannot possibly be the case because He is perfect. And since He is perfect He has no needs or limitations. He has no need for us, or for any other part of creation, to glorify Him.

7.   Actually, Lord, what St. Paul meant by giving glory to the Father, as You well know, is that all of creation to a lesser or greater

degree glorifies Him simply by sharing and reflecting His perfections.

8. As human beings we glorify God in our nature, especially with our intelligence and free will. But as Christians we glorify Him even more by reflecting His supernatural gifts, especially this gift of charity. Thus, the more like God we become, that is, the more charitable and selfless we become, the more we give glory to Him. When we glorify the Father in this manner, He is not the beneficiary, rather, we are. *(For more on glorifying God, see "The Catholic Catechism," pp. 82-83.)*

9. Lord, help us to glorify the Father more and more, and may we remember to offer thanks daily for all the natural and super- natural gifts He has given us. Most of all, through Your Holy Spirit inspire us to give thanks, especially at Mass for our salvation which You earned for us.

10.   Jesus, in chapter 2 of the Letter to the Ephesians, St. Paul speaks of people being dead through their sins.[102] He refers, of course, to mortal sins which prevent access to the Father's own divine life which He gives to those who truly love Him.

11.   Therefore, when we are denied entry into the divine life of the Father, we are spiritually dead and in danger of eternal damnation.

12. * Thankfully, Lord, You have suffered and died for us so that spiritual death need no longer be a reality for us. When we were baptized, we shared in Your victory over sin and we were spiritually reborn to share in Your divine life, putting our spiritual death behind us.

13.   What is more, even if we should become spiritually dead again through mortal sins committed after Baptism, You in Your magnificent charity have given us the sacrament of Penance. And it is through this sacrament that we can once more share in God's life and in the life of sanctifying grace which leads to holiness.

14.   Thank You, Lord, for Your infinite patience and mercy towards us. How unworthy we are of such loving attention. Also constantly remind us that one of the conditions for receiving Your forgiveness is to be forgiving and charitable towards those who have sinned against us.

15.   In closing, Lord, we want to share with

You thoughts which came to us while thinking about the last paragraph of today's Scripture reading.[104]

16.   St. Paul says that Gentile Christians, which includes most of us, are no longer separated from God's special providential concern. Thus, in the period of the Old Covenant the Jews were the special objects of God's providence to prepare for Your Coming. Now, in the era of the New Covenant, all of us, Jews and Gentiles alike, are called to share with You in the joy of Your Father's eternal Kingdom.

17.   Most Merciful Messiah, help us to spread the Good News of the Kingdom to non-Christians and to non-practicing Christians. And constantly remind us that the fullness of Your Kingdom on earth can be found only in the Church of which You are the invisible Head. Therefore, help us to take advantage of opportunities to introduce all of our neighbors to the glories of Your Church. And assist us in becoming its worthy representatives. Amen.

Try to read these Scripture passages and meditations in a reflective manner every day. The Holy Spirit will reveal more insights to you each time you do so.

Please read and meditate on Chapter XII, Paragraphs 1 to 8; Chapter XIII, Paragraphs 1 to 3; and Chapter XIV, Paragraphs 1 to 12 in our "Prayers and Recommended Practices" book.

Paul, a servant of the mystery (C4)

1 **3** So I, Paul, a prisoner of Christ Jesus for
2 the sake of you pagans . . . •You have
probably heard how I have been entrusted by
3 God with the grace he meant for you, •and
that it was by a revelation that I was given
the knowledge of the mystery, as I have just
4 described it very shortly. •If you read my
words, you will have some idea of the depths
5 that I see in the mystery of Christ. •This mystery that has now been revealed through the
Spirit to his holy apostles and prophets was
6 unknown to any men in past generations; •it
means that pagans now share the same inheritance, that they are parts of the same body,
and that the same promise has been made to
them, in Christ Jesus, through the gospel.

7 I have been made the servant of that gospel
by a gift of grace from God who gave it to
8 me by his own power. •I, who am less than
the least of all the saints, have been entrusted
with this special grace, not only of proclaiming to the pagans the infinite treasure of
9 Christ •but also of explaining how the mys-

tery is to be dispensed. Through all the ages, this has been kept hidden in God, the creator
10 of everything. Why? •So that the Sovereignties and Powers should learn only now, through the Church, how comprehensive
11 God's wisdom really is, •exactly according to the plan which he had had from all eternity
12 in Christ Jesus our Lord. •This is why we are bold enough to approach God in complete (C1)
13 confidence, through our faith in him; •so, I (C1) beg you, never lose confidence just because of the trials that I go through on your ac- (C3) count: they are your glory.

Paul's prayer

14   This, then, is what I pray, kneeling be-
15 fore the Father, •from whom every family, (C3) whether spiritual or natural, takes its name:
16   Out of his infinite glory, may he give you the power through his Spirit for your hidden
17 self to grow strong, •so that Christ may live (C1) in your hearts through faith, and then, planted (C3)
18 in love and built on love, •you will with all the saints have strength to grasp the breadth and the length, the height and the depth;
19 until, knowing the love of Christ, which is beyond all knowledge, you are filled with the utter fullness of God.
20   Glory be to him whose power, working in us, can do infinitely more than we can ask or
21 imagine; •glory be to him from generation to generation in the Church and in Christ Jesus for ever and ever. Amen.

II. EXHORTATION

A call to unity

1 **4** I, the prisoner in the Lord, implore you therefore to lead a life worthy of your vo- (C3)
2 cation. •Bear with one another charitably, in (C4) complete selflessness, gentleness and pa- (C3)
3 tience. •Do all you can to preserve the unity

205

of the Spirit by the peace that binds you ^(C3)
4 together. ·There is one Body, one Spirit, just
as you were all called into one and the same
5 hope when you were called. ·There is one
6 Lord, one faith, one baptism, ·and one God ^(C1)
who is Father of all, over all, through all and
within all.

7 Each one of us, however, has been given
his own share of grace, given as Christ allot-
8 ted it. ·It was said that he would:

*When he ascended to the height, he captured
prisoners,
he gave gifts to men.^a*

9 When it says, "he ascended," what can it
mean if not that he descended right down to

10 the lower regions of the earth? ·The one who
rose higher than all the heavens to fill all
things is none other than the one who de-
11 scended. ·And to some, his gift was that they
should be apostles; to some, prophets; to

some, evangelists; to some, pastors and
12 teachers; •so that the saints together make a
unity in the work of service, building up the
13 body of Christ. •In this way we are all to
come to unity in our faith and in our knowledge of the Son of God, until we become the
perfect Man, fully mature with the fullness
of Christ himself.

14   Then we shall not be children any longer,
or tossed one way and another and carried (C2)
along by every wind of doctrine, at the mercy
of all the tricks men play and their cleverness (C1)
15 in practicing deceit. •If we live by the truth
and in love, we shall grow in all ways into (C3)
16 Christ, who is the head •by whom the whole
body is fitted and joined together, every joint
adding its own strength, for each separate
part to work according to its function. So the
body grows until it has built itself up, in love. (C3)

17 In particular, I want to urge you in the name of the Lord, not to go on living the (C2)
18 aimless kind of life that pagans live. •Intellectually they are in the dark, and they are estranged from the life of God, without knowledge because they have shut their hearts to (C2)
19 it. •Their sense of right and wrong once (C2) dulled, they have abandoned themselves to sexuality and eagerly pursue a career of inde-
20 cency of every kind. •Now that is hardly the
21 way you have learned from Christ, •unless
. you failed to hear him properly when you
22 were taught what the truth is in Jesus. •You (C2) must give up your old way of life; you must put aside your old self, which gets corrupted
23 by following illusory desires. •Your mind must be renewed by a spiritual revolution (C3)
24 so that you can put on the new self that has been created in God's way, in the goodness and holiness of the truth.

25 So from now on, there must be no more (C2) lies: *You must speak the truth to one another,*[b] (C3)
26 since we are all parts of one another. •*Even if you are angry, you must not sin:*[c] never let
27 the sun set on your anger •or else you will (C2)
28 give the devil a foothold. •Anyone who was a thief must stop stealing; he should try to (C2) find some useful manual work instead, and (C3) be able to do some good by helping others (C2)
29 that are in need. •Guard against foul talk; let (C3) your words be for the improvement of others, as occasion offers, and do good to your lis-
30 teners, •otherwise you will only be grieving (C2) the Holy Spirit of God who has marked you with his seal for you to be set free when the
31 day comes. •Never have grudges against oth- (C2) ers, or lose your temper, or raise your voice (C2) to anybody, or call each other names, or al-
32 low any sort of spitefulness. •Be friends with (C3) one another, and kind, forgiving each other as readily as God forgave you in Christ.

Week 3 Day 4
Four C's Meditations
on Ephesians 3:1-4:32

1. Jesus, Our Redeemer, we observed in today's reading that St. Paul describes himself as a prisoner. But even in prison he did not cease his concern for Jews and Gentiles alike, longing to bring them to You through Your Church. *(St. Paul was a prisoner in Rome.)*

2. While in prison St. Paul evangelized by letter. And on at least one occasion, he preached the Gospel to a jailer and his household. In another instance, while under guard he preached openly in Rome to all who would listen. [105]

3. Elsewhere, Lord, we commented on the great difficulties and sufferings which St. Paul experienced in order to bring the Gospel to his fellow man. [106] Yet, in spite of these, he describes himself in today's meditation as "less than the least of all the saints." [107] This might seem like false humility, but it really is not. Let's examine another statement of his

along these same lines for further evidence in the matter.

4. In I Corinthians 15:9, St. Paul claims he was "the least of the Apostles" because as a non-Christian he had persecuted the Church. In other words, he saw himself completely unworthy of the many graces You bestowed upon him, including that of being an Apostle. True, he also claims to have worked hard and to have received divine favors, but this he says was due in the first place to the free, unmerited gift of Your grace. [108]

5. "I am the least of the apostles; in fact, since I persecuted the Church of God, I hardly deserve the name apostle; but by God's grace, that is what I am, and the grace he gave me has not been fruitless. On the contrary, I, or rather the grace of God that is with me, have worked harder than any of the others . . ." [109]

6. What we are seeing displayed then, Lord, is really true humility. St. Paul did not deny that by cooperating with Your grace, merited for him on the Cross, he accomplished great things, but he knew that he had been a great sinner, more so than others. And if it had not been for You, he rightly maintains he would have accomplished absolutely nothing.

7. Jesus, Our God and Creator, we, like Paul, should always acknowledge our great indebtedness to You for all You have given us and for all the good we have achieved. As a matter of fact we would not even be alive if it

weren't for Your providential love for us. This is made clear by St. Paul's own words when he said that it is in God "that we live, and move, and exist."[110] Moreover, St. Paul notes that all we have comes from You. "What do you have that was not given to you? And if it was given, how can you boast as if it were not?[111] We can do absolutely nothing without Your constant help, whether it is on the natural or supernatural levels of our existence.

8.   Unfortunately, Lord, at times we are too ready to take credit for our good deeds and too hesitant to admit our sins and faults. Please help us to be more mindful of Your providential action in our lives and to confess in humility our sinfulness which hinders Your work of salvation for all mankind.

9.   Lord, we also noted with interest St. Paul's explicit reference to the complete confidence (trust) he had in the Father. And he urged his readers never to lose their confidence in Him as a result of "the trials that I go through on your account: (actually) they are your glory."[112]

10.   May we always have complete confidence in the Father, and in You and in the Holy Spirit when we suffer various trials and temptations. And may we maintain our confidence even when we see the innocent suffer. Thus, may we never conclude that because we and others sometimes experience suffering that God must not care for people or that He must not exist. Actually, our

sufferings as Christians constitute the crosses we must bear in order to be found worthy of the Kingdom of God. [113]

11.   Always impress upon us too, Lord, Your words of comfort when You said, "Come to me, all of you who labor and are overburdened and I will give you rest." Also remind us always of Your promise to be with Your followers to the end of the world. [114]

12.   In chapter four of Ephesians, Jesus, St. Paul urges his readers to avoid sin and to live in truth and in charity. And we would like to add that by doing so people acquire not only sanctity for themselves, but they help make reparation for the sins of the world.

13.   Thank You, Jesus, for allowing us to share in Your work of reparation through our sufferings and acts of charity. Please inspire us to continue sacrificing ourselves willingly for the sake of others, especially for those in most need of Your love and forgiveness. And give us the grace to persevere in these efforts, even when we encounter apparent failure

and rejection. Thus, may many be brought to the light of Your everlasting truth and love. Amen.

Re-read and re-meditate on these Scripture passages and reflections at least one more time today.

Please read and meditate on Chapter XIV, Paragraphs 13 to 35 in our "Prayers and Recommended Practices" book.

WEEK 3 DAY 5
Ephesians 5:1-6:24

1 **5** Try, then, to imitate God, as children of (C3)
2 his that he loves, •and follow Christ by (C3)
loving as he loved you, giving himself up in (C3)
our place *as a fragrant offering and a sacri-*
3 *fice to God.ª* •Among you there must be not
even a mention of fornication or impurity in (C2)
any of its forms, or promiscuity: this would (C2)
4 hardly become the saints! •There must be no (C2)
coarseness, or salacious talk and jokes—all
this is wrong for you; raise your voices in
5 thanksgiving instead. •For you can be quite (C3)
certain that nobody who actually indulges in (C2)
fornication or impurity or promiscuity—
which is worshiping a false god—can inherit

6 anything of the kingdom of God. ·Do not let anyone deceive you with empty arguments: (C2) it is for this loose living that God's anger (C2) comes down on those who rebel against him.
7 Make sure that you are not included with
8 them. ·You were darkness once, but now you (C2) are light in the Lord; be like children of light,
9 for the effects of the light are seen in com- (C3) plete goodness and right living and truth.
10 Try to discover what the Lord wants of you, (C3)
11 having nothing to do with the futile works of (C2)
12 darkness but exposing them by contrast. ·The (C2) things which are done in secret are things that
13 people are ashamed even to speak of; ·but anything exposed by the light will be il-
14 luminated ·and anything illuminated turns into light. That is why it is said:[b]

Wake up from your sleep, (C1)
rise from the dead, (C2)
and Christ will shine on you. (C3)

15 So be very careful about the sort of lives you (C3) lead, like intelligent and not like senseless (C2)
16 people. ·This may be a wicked age, but your (C2)
17 lives should redeem it. ·And do not be (C3) thoughtless but recognize what is the will of
18 the Lord. ·Do not drug yourselves with wine, (C2) this is simply dissipation; be filled with the
19 Spirit. ·Sing the words and tunes of the Psalms and hymns when you are together, and go on singing and chanting to the Lord (C3)
20 in your hearts, ·so that always and every- (C3) where you are giving thanks to God who is our Father in the name of our Lord Jesus Christ.

The morals of the home

21 Give way to one another in obedience to (C3)
22 Christ. ·Wives should regard their husbands (C3)
23 as they regard the Lord, ·since as Christ is head of the Church and saves the whole body, so is a husband the head of his wife:
24 and as the Church submits to Christ, so (C3)

should wives to their husbands, in every-

25 thing. •Husbands should love their wives just (C3)
as Christ loved the Church and sacrificed

26 himself for her •to make her holy. He made
her clean by washing her in water with a form

27 of words, •so that when he took her to himself (C3)
she would be glorious, with no speck or wrin-
kle or anything like that, but holy and fault-

28 less. •In the same way, husbands must love (C3)
their wives as they love their own bodies; for (C3)
a man to love his wife is for him to love

29 himself. •A man never hates his own body, (C3)
but he feeds it and looks after it; and that is (C2)

30 the way Christ treats the Church, •because
it is his body—and we are its living parts.

31 *For this reason, a man must leave his father
and mother and be joined to his wife, and the*

32 *two will become one body.*c •This mystery has
many implications; but I am saying it applies

33 to Christ and the Church. •To sum up; you
too, each one of you, must love his wife as (C3)
he loves himself; and let every wife respect (C3)
her husband.

1 **6**Children, be obedient to your parents in
2 the Lord—that is your duty. •The first (C3)
commandment that has a promise attached to (C3)

3 it is: *Honor your father and mother,* •and the
promise is: *and you will prosper and have a*

4 *long life in the land.*a •And parents, never (C2)
drive your children to resentment but in

215

bringing them up correct them and guide (C 3)
them as the Lord does.

5 Slaves, be obedient to the men who are called your masters in this world, with deep respect and sincere loyalty, as you are obedi-
6 ent to Christ: ·not only when you are under their eye, as if you had only to please men, but because you are slaves of Christ and (C3)
7 wholeheartedly do the will of God. ·Work hard and willingly, but do it for the sake of (C3)
8 the Lord and not for the sake of men. ·You can be sure that everyone, whether a slave or a free man, will be properly rewarded by the Lord for whatever work he has done well. (C3)
9 And those of you who are employers, treat (C3) your slaves in the same spirit; do without threats, remembering that they and you have the same Master in heaven and he is not (C2) impressed by one person more than by another.

The spiritual war

10 Finally, grow strong in the Lord, with the (C1)
11 strength of his power. ·Put God's armor on (C2)

so as to be able to resist the devil's tactics. (C3)
12 For it is not against human enemies that we (C4) have to struggle, but against the Sovereignties and the Powers who originate the dark- (C2) ness in this world, the spiritual army of evil
13 in the heavens. ·That is why you must rely (C1) on God's armor, or you will not be able to put up any resistance when the worst hap- (C2) pens, or have enough resources to hold your (C1) ground.
14 So stand your ground, with *truth buckled* (C2) *round your waist,* and *integrity for a breast-* (C3)
15 *plate,*[b] ·wearing for shoes on your feet *the* (C4)
16 *eagerness to spread the gospel of peace*[c] ·and (C1) always carrying the shield of faith so that you can use it to put out the burning arrows of
17 the evil one. ·And then you must accept *salvation from God to be your helmet* and re-

216

ceive the word of God from the Spirit to use as a sword.

18 Pray all the time, asking for what you need, praying in the Spirit on every possible occa- (C3) sion. Never get tired of staying awake to pray (C3)
19 for all the saints; ·and pray for me to be given (C3) an opportunity to open my mouth and speak without fear and give out the mystery of the
20 gospel ·of which I am an ambassador in chains; pray that in proclaiming it I may speak as boldly as I ought to. (C3)

Personal news and final salutation

21 I should like you to know, as well, what is happening to me and what I am doing; my dear brother Tychicus, my loyal helper in the
22 Lord, will tell you everything. ·I am sending him to you precisely for this purpose, to give you news about us and reassure you.

23 May God the Father and the Lord Jesus (C3) Christ grant peace, love and faith to all the (C1)
24 brothers. ·May grace and eternal life be with (C3) all who love our Lord Jesus Christ.

Week 3 Day 5
Four C's Meditations
on Ephesians 5:1-6:24

1. Jesus, Our Savior, in the very first sentence of today's Scripture reading St. Paul provides a prescription for Christian living. "Try, then, to imitate God as children of his that he loves, and follow Christ by loving him as he has loved you, giving himself up in our place as a fragrant offering and a sacrifice to God."(115)

2. We are to imitate God. And since You, Lord, are God we are to imitate You. One way we can do this is by sowing seeds of self-sacrifice for others. This reminds us, Lord, of Your own words when You said, "I give you a new commandment: love one another; just as I have loved you, you also must love one another."(116)

3. Lord, every day there are opportunities for most of us to deny ourselves in order to help others. We can, for example, comfort the sick and the suffering. Also, there are a great many lonely people, especially among the elderly, who could benefit greatly from our acts of self-sacrifice. Simply a kind word or short greeting to people we meet on the street or on the bus or subway, for example, cannot help but improve our world, if only momentarily.

4. Savior, through Your Holy Spirit inspire us to see the needs of others in our daily lives so that we can sow seeds of charity for them, particularly for our own families.

5. There are those moments, too, when someone's needs are so great that much time and effort may be required of us. So much so, that it will seriously hurt us in one way or another. But to spend ourselves for them in Your Name is to demonstrate genuine charity, not only for them but for You also. As You once said, "Insofar as you did this to one of the least of these brothers of mine, you did it to me."[117]

6. Please, Jesus, inspire us to sacrifice ourselves for the needy in whatever way we can. And may we do so out of deep gratitude for all You have done for us and will continue to do for us.

7. Yesterday, Lord, we were meditating on making reparation for the sins of the world. Today, St. Paul mentions a similar idea when he says, "This may be a wicked age, but our lives should redeem it."[118] In other words, by our good works performed in the state of grace, we snatch from the devil, so to speak, a portion of our contemporary world which rightfully belongs to You as Creator and Ruler of creation.

8. How much evil there is in our society today! And how comforting to know, Lord, that our good works done in charity will help correct the horrible imbalance that evil has brought into the world.

9. Next, Lord we concentrated on that beautiful passage in which St. Paul compares the love husbands should have for their wives and the sacrificial love You have for Your Mystical Bride, the Church. Just as You sacrifice Yourself for Your Church to make it holy, so husbands must sacrifice themselves for their wives. [119]

10. Nonetheless, Jesus, some husbands, while expecting self-sacrifice from their wives, remain unwilling to reciprocate. The end result of this state of affairs is frequently lonely and unhappy wives.

11. Lord, help husbands to remember often Your generous love for Your Church. And remind them that their wives really require a special charity from them, which to neglect would be to imperil the unity and stability of the marriage bond.

12. St. Paul also has an important lesson for wives. Wives, he says, are to regard their husbands as having authority over them. This basic truth is too frequently overlooked or denied today. However, it is often misunderstood as well. While the husband is the head of his wife and the entire family, he must therefore be the most accountable member of the family. Moreover, his attitude towards his

wife must be one of tenderness and loving concern, and not that of a tyrant.

13. On the other hand, the wife in her role as the heart of the family is to be submissive to the legitimate requests of the family's head. Obviously, she must not submit to him when he requests or demands things that are sinful. And she should not be treated as a child or a slave, but as a loving partner.

14. Thankfully, Lord, as many of us know from experience, if husbands and wives would turn to You together in prayer daily, little or no friction will occur between the head of the family and the beloved spouse, since You are the Source of family unity and stability.

15.   Jesus, St. Paul also cautions children to be obedient to their parents, since it is their duty. To do otherwise, would be to promote family disunity, thus harming the basic cells of Your Mystical Body. St. Paul points out that obedient children will, in effect, be happy children rewarded by God. Children who are obedient sacrifice themselves for the good of the family and therefore help build up and strengthen the Church. St. Paul also warned parents not to drive their children to resentment. Rather, they are to be corrected and guided in the spirit of seed-charity.

16.   Jesus, Mary and Joseph, as families turn to You daily in prayer, bless and watch over them. May family members never harbor resentment or bitterness for one another. But when these exist, help the guilty quickly to repent and seek the forgiveness of those whom they have offended. Especially, help parents to be models of mutual charity for the sake of their children, thus preparing them for the time when they may also be sharing in the blessings and responsibilities of the sacrament of Marriage.

17.   Finally, Lord, St. Paul completes his letter by noting that Christians must, in the last analysis, struggle not against human enemies, but against the spiritual enemies of satan's kingdom. Consequently, he warns that spiritual weapons are necessary for our combat against evil; weapons such as faith, truth, integrity, and the "eagerness to spread the gospel of peace."[120]

18.   Undergirding the use of these weapons, St. Paul stresses the exercise of prayer. We are, he says, to pray constantly in the Holy Spirit asking for whatever we need to wage our battle against sin.

19.   Lord, we can never thank You enough for providing us with so much assistance in overcoming the forces of evil which seek to bring us to the very depths of hell. May we always avail ourselves of these weapons by exercising constant prayer. Thus, may the awesome forces of the evil one be finally eliminated from our lives. Amen.

The more you re-read these Scriptures and meditations, the more you will get out of them.

Please read and meditate on Chapter XV, Paragraphs 1 to 9 in or "Prayers and Recommended practices" book.

Philippians

THE LETTER OF PAUL
TO THE CHURCH
AT PHILIPPI

Address

1 **1** From Paul and Timothy, servants of
Christ Jesus, to all the saints in Christ
Jesus, together with their presiding elders (C3)
2 and deacons. ·We wish you the grace and
peace of God our Father and of the Lord
Jesus Christ.

Thanksgiving and prayer

3   I thank my God whenever I think of you; (C3)
4 and ·every time I pray for all of you, I pray
5 with joy, ·remembering how you have helped (C3)
to spread the Good News from the day you
6 first heard it right up to the present. ·I am
quite certain that the One who began this
good work in you will see that it is finished
7 when the Day of Christ Jesus comes. ·It is
only natural that I should feel like this towards you all, since you have shared the (C4)
privileges which have been mine: both my (C3)
chains and my work defending and establishing the gospel. You have a permanent place
8 in my heart, ·and God knows how much I (C3)
miss you all, loving you as Christ Jesus loves (C3)
9 you. ·My prayer is that your love for each
other may increase more and more and never (C4)
stop improving your knowledge and deepen- (C1)
10 ing your perception ·so that you can always (C2)
recognize what is best. This will help you to
become pure and blameless, and prepare you

11 for the Day of Christ, •when you will reach the perfect goodness which Jesus Christ produces in us for the glory and praise of God.

Paul's own circumstances

12   I am glad to tell you, brothers, that the tings that happen to me have actually been a help to the Good News.

13   My chains, in Christ, have become famous not only all over the Praetorium but every-
14 where, •and most of the brothers have taken courage in the Lord from these chains of mine and are getting more and more daring (C3) in announcing the Message without any fear. (C4)
15 It is true that some of them are doing it just out of rivalry and competition, but the rest (C2)
16 preach Christ with the right intention, •out of nothing but love, as they know that this is my (C3)
17 invariable way of defending the gospel. •The others, who proclaim Christ for jealous or selfish motives, do not mind if they make my (C2)
18 chains heavier to bear. •But does it matter? Whether from dishonest motives or in sincer- (C2) ity, Christ is proclaimed; and that makes me (C3)
19 happy; •and I shall continue being happy, be- cause I know *this will help to save me,*ᵃ thanks to your prayers and to the help which will be given to me by the Spirit of Jesus. (C3)

20 My one hope and trust is that I shall never (C1) have to admit defeat, but that now as always (C4) I shall have the courage for Christ to be glori- fied in my body, whether by my life or by my
21 death. •Life to me, of course, is Christ, but (C3) then death would bring me something more:
22 but then again, if living in this body means (C3) doing work which is having good results—I
23 do not know what I should choose. •I am caught in this dilemma: I want to be gone and be with Christ, which would be very much
24 the better, •but for me to stay alive in this (C3) body is a more urgent need for your sake.

225

25 This weighs with me so much that I feel sure
I shall survive and stay with you all, and help (C3)
you to progress in the faith and even increase
26 your joy in it; •and so you will have another (C3)
reason to give praise to Christ Jesus on my
account when I am with you again.

Fight for the faith

27   Avoid anything in your everyday lives that (C2)
would be unworthy of the gospel of Christ,
so that, whether I come to you and see for
myself, or stay at a distance and only hear (C1)
about you, I shall know that you are unani-
mous in meeting the attack with firm resist- (C1)
ance, united by your love for the faith of the (C3)
28 gospel •and quite unshaken by your enemies. (C2)
This would be the sure sign that they will lose
and you will be saved. It would be a sign from
29 God •that he has given you the privilege
not only of believing in Christ, but of suf- (C1)
30 fering for him as well. •You and I are to-- (C3)
gether in the same fight as you saw me fight- (C3)
ing before and, as you will have heard, I am (C4)
fighting still.

Preserve unity in humility

1 2 If our life in Christ means anything to you, (C3)
    if love can persuade at all, or the Spirit that

we have in common, or any tenderness and (C1)
2 sympathy, ·then be united in your convictions (C3)
and united in your love, with a common purpose and a common mind. That is the one
thing which would make me completely (C2)
3 happy. ·There must be no competition among (C3)
you, no conceit; but everybody is to be self- (C3)
effacing. Always consider the other person
4 to be better than yourself, ·so that nobody (C2)
thinks of his own interests first but everybody (C3)
5 thinks of other people's interests instead. ·In
your minds you must be the same as Christ
Jesus:[a]

6   His state was divine,
       yet he did not cling
       to his equality with God
7   but emptied himself
       to assume the condition of a slave,
       and became as men are;
       and being as all men are,
8   he was humbler yet,
       even to accepting death,

       death on a cross.
9   But God raised him high
       and gave him the name
       which is above all other names
10   so that *all beings*

in the heavens, on earth and in the under-
world,

should bend the knee[b] at the name of Jesus
11 and that every tongue should acclaim
Jesus Christ as Lord,
to the glory of God the Father.

Work for salvation

12 So then, my dear friends, continue to do (C3)
as I tell you, as you always have; not only as
you did when I was there with you, but even (C4)
more now that I am no longer there; and
work for your salvation "in fear and trem (C1)
13 bling." ·It is God, for his own loving purpose, (C2)
                                              (C3)
who puts both the will and the action into (C4)
14 you. ·Do all that has to be done without com- (C3)
15 plaining or arguing ·and then you will be innocent and genuine, *perfect children of God* (C2)
among a deceitful and underhand brood,[c] and (C3)
you will shine in the world like bright stars (C2)
16 because you are offering it the word of life.
This would give me something to be proud
of for the Day of Christ, and would mean that
I had not run in the race and exhausted my- (C3)
17 self for nothing. ·And then, if my blood has (C4)
to be shed as part of your own sacrifice and
offering—which is your faith[d]—I shall still (C3)
18 be happy and rejoice with all of you, ·and (C1)
you must be just as happy and rejoice with
me.

The mission of Timothy and Epaphroditus

19 I hope, in the Lord Jesus, to send Timothy
to you soon, and I shall be reassured by hav-
20 ing news of you. ·I have nobody else like him
here, as wholeheartedly concerned for your (C3)
21 welfare: ·all the rest seem more interested in (C2)
22 themselves than in Jesus Christ. ·But you
know how he has proved himself by working (C3)
with me on behalf of the Good News like a (C4)
23 son helping his father. ·That is why he is the
one that I am hoping to send you, as soon
as I know something definite about my fate. (C3)

24 But I continue to trust, in the Lord, that I (C1)
shall be coming soon myself.

25 It is essential, I think, to send brother Epaphroditus back to you. He was sent as your (C3)
representative to help me when I needed
someone to be my companion in working and (C3)

26 battling, ·but he misses you all and is worried

27 because you heard about his illness. ·It is true
that he has been ill, and almost died, but God
took pity on him, and on me as well as him,
and spared me what would have been one

28 grief on top of another. ·So I shall send him
back as promptly as I can; you will be happy (C3)
to see him again, and that will make me less

29 sorry. ·Give him a most hearty welcome, in (C3)
the Lord; people like him are to be honored.

30 It was for Christ's work that he came so near
to dying, and he risked his life to give me the
help that you were not able to give me yourselves.

Week 3 Day 6
Four C's Meditations
on Philippians 1:1-2:30

1. Lord, in St. Paul's letter to the Church at
Philippi we see reflected the immense love he
had for the Philippian Christians. They
obviously were a joy for him and apparently

had given him few, if any, reasons for serious concern about their spiritual well-being. *(Be sure to read the introductory remarks about this letter found in paragraphs 76-78 of the introduction of this book.)*

2. As their spiritual father, St. Paul encouraged them to remain steadfast in the Catholic Faith he had given them, and he cautioned them against falling into sin. Undoubtedly, the doctrinal and moral trouble he was having at the same time with the Corinthian Christians colored his thinking here. That is, he wanted the Philippians to avoid falling into the same errors and problems which were then tormenting the Corinthian Church.

3. Jesus, we noted with interest in today's meditation several references to prayer. Volumes have already been written on this subject and we don't intend to dwell too long on it here. But the prayers of Your friends are powerful instruments for the salvation and sanctification of the entire world.

4. Thank You, Jesus, for Your gift of prayer whereby we can communicate with You, receive Your comforting graces, grow in sanctity, and accomplish immeasurable good for others.

5. Jesus, we noted also in today's meditation that St. Paul said his prison chains had encouraged most of the Christians familiar with his imprisonment to proclaim the Gospel without fear. But as You well know, it was not literally his chains that encouraged Paul's

fellow Christians, rather it was his witness to You while he was in chains.

6.   Lord, grant that we may constantly bear witness to You and Your Catholic Faith when we are burdened with trials and torments. In this way, our fellow Christians will be spiritually strengthened, and non-Christians will be attracted to Your Holy Catholic Church.

7.   Most Holy Savior, in today's reading, our attention was drawn to that well-known dilemma encountered by St. Paul. He was torn between his great desire to be with You in Heaven and the love he had for the Philippians who would profit from his support if he remained on earth.

8.   "I want to be gone and be with Christ, which would be very much the better, but for me to stay alive in this body is a more urgent need for your sake. This weighs with me so much that I feel sure I shall survive and stay with you all, and help you to progress in the faith and even increase in your joy in it . . ."[121]

9.   Most Sacred Heart of Jesus, we wish we were also at that point in our spiritual journey on earth where we would have so much love for You that we could hardly wait to be with You in Heaven seeing You "face to face!"[122] Most of us, however, rarely think about or even want to think about our possible existence with You in Heaven. *(See "The Catholic Catechism," pp. 260-263; 271-272 for more about being "face to face" with God, i.e., enjoying the Beatific Vision.)*

10. Whatever our condition is in this world, no matter how many difficulties we face, most of us are generally content with life on this planet. And we live as if there will be no other life than the here and now, although our Faith informs us to the contrary. The only remedy for this, Jesus, is to love You increasingly through a total surrender of ourselves to You, just as St. Paul did. Then the world, as good as it is in itself, will no longer have such a hold on us. Rather, we will be drawn to You with great fervor, longing to be with You constantly and anticipating that moment of eternal joy when we shall see You face to face in Heaven.

11. The amazing thing too, Lord, is that the more we love You the more we will love our fellow humans, especially our acquaintances and those closest to us. And as our charity increases for both You and others, we may also find ourselves torn at some point between seeing You face to face and sacrificing ourselves for others here on earth.

12. Finally, Jesus, we dwelled on that memorable passage in which St. Paul describes Your unsurpassed humility.[123] You Who are God, You Who owe us sinners nothing, for the sake of our salvation humbled Yourself to become one of us, and voluntarily accepted death on the Cross. "A man can have no greater love than to lay down his life for his friends."[124] But You, Jesus, are not only man, but God. Thus Your sacrifice for us reflects the seed-charity of God as well as of man. Please help us to imitate that same seed-charity for God and for man in our thoughts, words and deeds. Amen.

May the Holy Spirit allow you to experience the gift of God's peace by slowly re-reading and re-meditating on the Scripture for today.

Please read and meditate on Chapter XVI, Paragraphs 1 to 2 in our "Prayers and Recommended Practices" book.

1 **3** Finally, my brothers, rejoice in the Lord.*a* (C3)

The true way of Christian salvation

It is no trouble to me to repeat what I have already written to you, and as far as you are 2 concerned, it will make for safety. •Beware (C2) of dogs! Watch out for the people who are making mischief. Watch out for the cutters.*b* 3 We are the real people of the circumcision, we who worship in accordance with the Spirit of God; we have our own glory from Christ Jesus without having to rely on a physical 4 operation. •If it came to relying on physical evidence, I should be fully qualified myself. Take any man who thinks he can rely on what 5 is physical: I am even better qualified. •I was born of the race of Israel and of the tribe of Benjamin, a Hebrew born of Hebrew parents, and I was circumcised when I was eight days 6 old. As for the Law, I was a Pharisee; •as for working for religion, I was a persecutor of the Church; as far as the Law can make you 7 perfect, I was faultless. •But because of Christ, I have come to consider all these ad-

8 vantages that I had as disadvantages. •Not only that, but I believe nothing can happen (C1) that will outweigh the supreme advantage of knowing Christ Jesus my Lord. For him I (C2) have accepted the loss of everything, and I (C3) look on everything as so much rubbish if only (C4)

9 I can have Christ •and be given a place in him. I am no longer trying for perfection by my own efforts, the perfection that comes from

the Law, but I want only the perfection that (C1) comes through faith in Christ, and is from (C1) 10 God and based on faith. •All I want is to

234

know Christ and the power of his resurrection and to share his sufferings by reproduc- (C3)
11 ing the pattern of his death. •That is the way (C1)
I can hope to take my place in the resurrec-
12 tion of the dead. •Not that I have become
perfect yet: I have not yet won, but I am still (C4)
running, trying to capture the prize for which
13 Christ Jesus captured me. •I can assure you
my brothers, I am far from thinking that I
have already won. All I can say is that I forget (C3)
the past and I strain ahead for what is still to (C4)
14 come; •I am racing for the finish, for the prize
to which God calls us upward to receive in
15 Christ Jesus. •We who are called "perfect"
must all think in this way. If there is some
point on which you see things differently,
16 God will make it clear to you; •meanwhile, (C1)
let us go forward on the road that has brought (C2)
us to where we are.

17　My brothers, be united in following my (C2)
rule of life. Take as your models everybody (C4)
who is already doing this and study them as
18 you used to study us. •I have told you often,
and I repeat it today with tears, there are
many who are behaving as the enemies of the (C2)
19 cross of Christ. •They are destined to be lost.
They make foods into their god and they are (C2▸)
proudest of something they ought to think
shameful; the things they think important are
20 earthly things. •For us, our homeland is in
heaven, and from heaven comes the savior
we are waiting for, the Lord Jesus Christ,
21 and he will transfigure these wretched bodies
of ours into copies of his glorious body. He
will do that by the same power with which
he can subdue the whole universe.

1 **4** So then, my brothers and dear friends, do (C2)
not give way but remain faithful in the (C1)
Lord. I miss you very much, dear friends; you (C3)
are my joy and my crown.

Last advice

2　I appeal to Evodia and I appeal to Syn-

tyche to come to agreement with each other, (C3)
3 in the Lord; •and I ask you, Syzygus,^a to be (C1)
truly a "companion" and to help them in this.
These women were a help to me when I was
fighting to defend the Good News—and so, (C3)
at the same time, were Clement and the oth- (C3)
ers who worked with me. Their names are
written in the book of life.
4   I want you to be happy, always happy in
the Lord; I repeat, what I want is your happi- (C3)
5 ness. •Let your tolerance be evident to every-
6 one: the Lord is very near. •There is no need (C3)
to worry; but if there is anything you need,
pray for it, asking God for it with prayer and
7 thanksgiving, •and that peace of God, which
is so much greater than we can understand,
will guard your hearts and your thoughts, in (C1)
8 Christ Jesus. •Finally, brothers, fill your
minds with everything that is true, everything (C3)
that is noble, everything that is good and (C2)
pure, everything that we love and honor, and
everything that can be thought virtuous or
9 worthy of praise. •Keep doing all the things (C3)
that you learned from me and have been
taught by me and have heard or seen that
I do. Then the God of peace will be with
you.

10   It is a great joy to me, in the Lord, that at (C3)
last you have shown some concern for me
again; though of course you were concerned
11 before, and only lacked an opportunity. ·I am
not talking about shortage of money: I have
12 learned to manage on whatever I have, ·I (C4)
know how to be poor and I know how to be
rich too. I have been through my initiation
and now I am ready for anything anywhere:
full stomach or empty stomach, poverty or
13 plenty. ·There is nothing I cannot master (C4)
with the help of the One who gives me (C3)
14 strength. ·All the same, it was good of you
15 to share with me in my hardships. ·In the
early days of the Good News, as you people
of Philippi well know, when I left Macedonia,
no other church helped me with gifts of
16 money. You were the only ones; ·and twice (C3)
since my stay in Thessalonika you have sent
17 me what I needed. ·It is not your gift that I (C3)
value; what is valuable to me is the interest
18 that is mounting up in your account. ·Now
for the time being I have everything that I
need and more: I am fully provided now that
I have received from Epaphroditus the offer- (C3)
ing that you sent, *a sweet fragrance*—the sacrifice that God accepts and finds pleasing.
19 In return my God will fulfill all your needs,
in Christ Jesus, as lavishly as only God can.
20 Glory to God, our Father, for ever and ever. (C3)
Amen.

Greetings and final wish

21   My greetings to every one of the saints in (C3)
Christ Jesus. The brothers who are with me
22 send their greetings. ·All the saints send their (C3)
greetings, especially those of the imperial (C3)
23 household.[b] ·May the grace of the Lord Jesus
Christ be with your spirit.

Week 3 Day 7
Four C's Meditations
on Philippians 3:1-4:23

1. Jesus, Our Merciful Savior, in today's meditation, St. Paul exhorts his readers to "rejoice in the Lord."[125] By this St. Paul meant that the Philippians were to joyfully express their selfless love for the Father and their gratitude for all He had done for them through You, His only Begotten Son. In another place, St. Paul urged his fellow Christians to sing and chant to God "in their hearts."[126] And again, he wrote, "With gratitude in your hearts sings psalms and hymns and inspired songs to God."[127]

2. These words impress us because many in our Anglo-Saxon culture, men especially, are unaccustomed to expressing their love for You in such an emotional manner. We love God with our minds and wills, but tend to be distrustful of our emotions and affections. Yet, we express ourselves emotionally, for example, for our favorite sports team and

may have no qualms about displays of emotion for our loved ones. Perhaps we hesitate to express our charity and gratitude emotionally for God, at least in part, because of the seemingly excessive display of emotion for You the Father and the Holy Spirit, evidenced by some non-Catholic Christians. Whatever the reason, there is no question that such emotional displays of love for God, encouraged by St. Paul, are in large measure absent from many of us.

3. What is remarkable about St. Paul's approval of rejoicing in the Lord with hymns, psalms, etc., is the fact that he was really a man of great intelligence, also possessing an iron will, qualities which are often regarded, today, as incompatible with displays of emotion. And You Yourself, the perfect man, wept and were moved with compassion for others. [128] In fact, we really should praise and love You, Lord, with our whole beings, and we can do this both passively and actively.

4.   We praise You passively by avoiding sin. When we keep our consciences pure, our bodies — including our minds and our wills — become well-ordered and consequently they reflect the orderliness and goodness of God. And we praise You actively, not only with our minds and wills, but also by expressions of enthusiasm (emotion). Certainly, such expressions should be under our control, but as we learn from St. Paul's writings, they too are pleasing to You Who are Our Lord and Our God.

5.   Jesus, our attention also dwelt on the following passage in today's reading.

6.   "I want you to be happy, always happy in the Lord; I repeat, what I want is your happiness. Let your tolerance be evident to everyone: the Lord is very near. There is no need to worry; but if there is anything you need, pray for it asking God for it with prayer and thanksgiving, and that peace of God, which is so much greater than we can understand, will guard your hearts and your thoughts."[129]

7.   St. Paul wanted his spiritual children to be happy, happy in the Lord. This wish contradicts the opinion that many have of Christianity being a joyless religion, one which demands much and rewards little.

8.   No, Lord, not only St. Paul, but You also want us to be happy, not only in Heaven but on earth as well. We can be happy in this life by living in You. And we accomplish this by keeping ourselves free from sin and by

planting seeds of charity for You and for our neighbors. So by remaining literally in Your very Being, we are living in the Source of all true happiness. Moreover, we have access to that "peace of God, which is so much greater than we can understand."[(130)]

9.   Even though You, Jesus, are the Source of all true happiness, we are tempted daily to look elsewhere for it. Why? Because to obtain it from You we must surrender ourselves, body and soul, to You and to Your will. And many of us are not willing to do it! So, we look elsewhere for a less demanding source of lasting happiness. But we will never find it. We will encounter only unhappiness.

10.   Lord, inspire us constantly to give ourselves unreservedly to You with the realization that the more we do so, the happier we will be.

11.   Our last thought in today's reading, Most Sacred Heart of Jesus, is centered on what spiritual writers call the virtue of detachment. St. Paul unquestionably had this gift as his own words indicate.

12.   "I have learned to manage on whatever I have, I know how to be poor and I know how to be rich too. I have been through my intiation and now I am ready for anything anywhere: full stomach or empty stomach, poverty or plenty. There is nothing I cannot master with the help of the One who gives me strength."[131]

13.   In essence, St. Paul was perfectly content to do Your will in the state he found himself. He was completely indifferent to whether he was sick or well, a prisoner or a free man, well-fed or starving, rich or poor. Why? Because he was supremely confident that You, being perfect Love, would meet his needs no matter what his circumstances.

14.   St. Paul's spirit of detachment also reflected his love for You. If he did not love You, he would have been unwilling to experience severe hardships, even though he was confident that You would meet his every need.

15.   We too, Lord Jesus, should with Your grace cultivate the gift of detachment. Thus, we will be ready to do anything and go anywhere for Your sake, and for the sake of those for whom You died on the Cross. Please grant that it may be so. Amen.

Try to read these Scripture passages and meditations several times a day in a reflective manner. Each time you do so, the Holy Spirit will give you more insights.

Please read and meditate on Chapter XVII, Paragraphs 1 to 8; and on Chapter XVIII, Paragraphs 1 to 2 in our "Prayers and Recommended Practices" book.

References to Scripture

(1) 2 Cor 11:21-28
(2) Acts 9:1-2, 2-4
(3) 2 Cor 1:23-24
(4) 1 Cor 1:18-31, 18:2:14
(5) 1 Cor 3:5-15
(6) Matthew 25:14-30
(7) Matthew 28:20
(8) 1 Cor 4:6
(9) 1 Cor 4:7
(10) 1 Cor 5:5
(11) 1 Cor 5:9-10
(12) Matthew 9:13
(13) John 17:15-16
(14) 1 Cor 6:12
(15 1 Cor 6:9-11
(16) 1 Cor 6:18-19; Mt 15:19
(17) 1 Cor 10:13
(18) 1 Cor 7:3
(19) 1 Cor 7:4-5
(20) 1 Cor 7:25-40
(21) 1 Cor 8:1-13
(22) 1 Cor 9:22-23
(23) 1 Cor 9:24-27
(24) 1 Cor 10:1-3
(25) 1 Cor 10:12
(26) Proverbs 16:18
(27) 1 Cor 10:14-22
(28) 1 Cor 10:2-16; 11:2-16
(29) 1 Cor 11:3
(30) 1 Cor 11:17-34
(31) 1 Cor 12:1-11
(32) Matthew 25:14-30
(33) 1 Cor 14:1
(34) 1 Cor 13:2
(35) 1 Cor 14:18-19

(36) 1 Cor 14:3
(37) Acts 4:1-22; 14:1-6, 19-20
(38) 1 Cor 15:14-19
(39) 1 Cor 16:1-4
(40) II Cor 1:3-7
(41) Col 1:24
(42) Matthew 11:28-30
(43) 2 Cor 1:5
(44) 2 Cor 1:3
(45) 2 Cor 2:6-8
(46) 2 Cor 3:4-13
(47) 2 Cor 4:13
(48) 2 Cor 3:6
(49) 2 Cor 3:18
(50) 2 Cor 4:2-3
(51) Matthew 28:20
(52) 2 Cor 4:17
(53) 1 Peter 4:12-14
(54) II Cor 5:1-10
(55) Matthew 10:37
(56) II Cor 4:17
(57) II Cor 5:10
(58) II Cor 5:14-15
(59) II Cor 6:1
(60) II Cor 5:3-10
(61) II Cor 7:1
(62) I Cor 16:1-4
(63) II Cor 8:1-5, 9-16
(64) Luke 21:1-4
(65) II Cor 9:5
(66) II Cor 8:9
(67) II Cor 8:12-13
(68) 2 Cor 9:6
(69) 2 Cor 9:8
(70) II Cor 10:3-4
(71) II Cor 10:6

(72) Matthew 20:25-28
(73) II Cor 11:4
(74) II Cor 11:16-32
(75) II Cor 12:9
(76) II Cor 12:9-10
(77) II Cor 13:3-4
(78) Matthew 5:48; II Corinthians 13:9, 11
(79) II Cor 12:20
(80) II Cor 12:21
(81) Gal 1:6
(82) Gal 2:15-16
(83) Acts 10:11
(84) Gal 2:11-13
(85) Acts 2-4
(86) Matthew 10:28
(87) Matthew 10:32-33
(88) Gal 2:15-21
(89) James 2:14-17
(90) 1 Cor 13:2-3
(91) John 15:5
(92) Gal 5:4-6
(93) Gal 5:19-22
(94) 1 Cor 6:19
(95) John 14:6
(96) Gal 5:22
(97) Gal 6:15
(98) II Cor 5:17
(99) Ph 4:7
(100) Ep 1:14
(101) Ep 1:12
(102) Ep 1:14
(103) Ep 2:5
(104) Ep 2:19-22
(105) Acts 28:16, 25-31
(106) 1 Cor 11:21-28
(107) Ep 3:8

(108) II Cor 11:23; 12:1-7; Acts 9:1-9
(109) I Cor 15:9-10 Gal 3:7
(110) Acts 17:28
(111) 1 Cor 4:7
(112) Ep 3:12-13
(113) 2 Th 1:5
(114) Matthew 28:20
(115) Ep 5:1
(116) John 13:34
(117) Matthew 25:40
(118) Ep 5:16
(119) Ep 5:25
(120) Ep 6:15
(121) Ph 1:23-25
(122) I Cor 13:12
(123) Ph 2:6-11
(124) John 15:13
(125) Ph 3:1
(126) Ep 5:19
(127) Col 3:16
(128) Matthew 9:30; 14:14
(129) Ph 4:4-7
(131) Ph 4:7
(131) Ph 4:11-14

The Work and Goals of the Apostolate

Purpose

The Apostolate for Family Consecration is an international community of believers whose specific purpose and unique role in the Church is to reinforce the Christian family through the systematic transformation of neighborhoods into God-centered communities. As a result of the establishment of enough of these "God-centered communities," a nation will advance significantly on the spiritual plane, and in most instances, even on the material level. "Virtue makes a nation great, by sin whole races are disgraced." *(Proverbs 14:34)* "Happy is the nation whose God is the Lord." *(Psalms 33:12)* "'...Bad friends ruin the noblest of people." *(I Cor. 15:33)*

Motto

All for the Sacred and Eucharistic Heart of Jesus, all through the Sorrowful and Immaculate Heart of Mary, all in union with St. Joseph.

Spirituality

The four biblical pillars of the Apostolate's "Peaceful Seed Living" spirituality are Confidence, Conscience, seed-Charity and Constancy. When a person builds his or her daily life on these four pillars, he or she will be living a life of true union with God and will be blessed with a peaceful heart that only God can give.

Spiritual Goal

Our spiritual goal is to develop a deep interior union with the Holy Spirit of God. The best way to achieve this mystical union is by increasing not the number of prayers said but the fervor and time invested in prayer and meditation every day. When we convert our daily trials encountered through the fulfillment of our responsibilities into sacrifices for God, we actually unite ourselves with Christ's sacrifice of the Mass at Calvary. Only through these spiritual means, can we restore man's relationship with God and loosen the diabolical hold the forces of evil have on so many families, schools, neighborhoods, our country and the entire world.

Act of Consecration

The Act of Total Consecration to the Holy Family which the Apostolate promotes, offers all of a person's spiritual and material possessions for the Sacred and Eucharistic Heart of Jesus, through the Sorrowful and Immaculate Heart of Mary, in union with St. Joseph.

Through this act of total consecration, individuals are asking to be purified and used as God's instruments by the Holy Family. It is recognized that the Holy Family can do far more good with people's humble possessions than they ever could on their own. We believe that this offering enables God to multiply an individual's merits and offset the effects of sin in the world. *(2 Cor. 9:10)*

People who are totally consecrated give all of their indulgences to the Holy Family to relieve the suffering of loved ones and other Poor Souls in Purgatory. The Poor Souls are asked to continually pray that all the members of our families and the members and families of the Apostolate fulfill, to the fullest extent, the Father's distinctive plan for their lives.

Our Cooperator, Chapter and Apostolic members are required to make this act of total consecration. Other members and individuals who participate in our "Neighborhood Peace of Heart Forums" are encouraged, but not required, to also totally consecrate themselves to the Holy Family.

The Church's Guide and Incentive for Holiness

The Apostolate uses the Church's norms for indulgences as a specific guide for achieving a balanced, God-centered life in the modern world, while asking its members to perform heroic acts of charity by giving their indulgences to the Poor Souls in purgatory.

Neighborhood Chapter Programs

Our goal, God willing, is to establish, within every nation, a national network of Neighborhood Chapters capable of continually educating and motivating people to place God first in their lives. These chapters will perform four distinct functions:

• Change personal attitudes of neighborhood residents through in-depth and continuous "Neighborhood Peace of Heart Forums."

• Deepen personal commitment and effectiveness through total consecration to the Holy Family through our home visitation programs.

• Consolidate neighborhoods through public devotions in our churches.

• Cultivate our youth through our youth leadership program.

When Chapters are Established

After enough Neighborhood Chapters are established in an area, the Apostolate will utilize the media as a positive means to draw people into our in-depth formation programs. We will also establish, within the area, a combination audio-visual lending library, religious book store and gift shop operated by our members.

Types of Membership

Membership is open to all who qualify and fulfill the following conditions:

A. Sacri-State members are those who offer up as a sacrifice of their state in life, their trials encountered in the faithful fulfillment of their responsibilities. They recognize the fact these sacrifices are not only meritorious, but if specifically willed, are also indulgenced by the Church.

Sacri-State members freely entrust either part or all of their merits and indulgences, earned from their prayers and sacrifices, to be distributed by the Holy Family. The Holy Family is asked to apply the merits of the members toward the work of the Apostolate, and to apply their indulgences for their loved ones and other Poor Souls in Purgatory.

We ask the Poor Souls helped by our indulgences to continually pray that all the members of our family and the members and families of the Apostolate fulfill the Father's distinctive plan for their lives. This commitment need only be made once and may be revoked by a specific act of the will at any time. Sacri-State members do not have to totally consecrate themselves to the Holy Family.

Sacri-State membership is a spiritual bond and, therefore, no formal application is necessary. One need only submit a note indicating a willingness to fulfill these conditions. There are also no dues for Sacri-State members.

If you belong to a religious community or an organized apostolic group, your entire community can join and become a Sacri-State community of the Apostolate.

B. Cooperator members are those who fulfill the conditions for Sacri-State membership, and also totally consecrate themselves to the Holy Family, and strive to follow the recommended practices, and recite the recommended prayers of the Apostolate for Family Consecration.

In addition, to become a Cooperator member, one should send for our formal application form and submit it for certification. Cooperator members may also be candidates for the following Apostolic or Chapter memberships.

C. Chapter members are those who are totally consecrated to the Holy Family and have successfully completed our candidate program, while actively working in the Apostolate on a voluntary basis.

D. Apostolic members are those who are totally consecrated to the Holy Family and have successfully completed our candidate program, while having committed themselves to devote at least one year in the work of the Apostolate on a full time basis.

E. Benefactor members are those individuals who contribute the much needed financial assistance to the Apostolate for Family Consecration. One may be a Benefactor member and also one of the other mentioned members.

Benefits of Membership

In unity there is strength. Our living and deceased members and their families will be remembered in all of the Masses offered for the Apostolate and its work.

In addition, all living and deceased members and their families will be remembered through the perpetual vigil lights in the sanctuary of the Sacred Hearts Chapel at the House of St. Joseph.

All members of the Apostolate are actually part of a community of believers who share in the prayers and merits of the other members throughout the world. We particularly ask our members to pray on Fridays for the specific petitions sent in to the Apostolate.

St. Paul said: "The more you sow, the more you reap." *(2 Cor. 9:6)* When you pray for others, you plant a seed of love that will bear an abundant harvest for your loved ones, yourselves and the entire Mystical Body of Christ.

All members who have been properly enrolled and wear the Brown Scapular, or Scapular medal of Our Lady of Mount Carmel, qualify for the Sabbatine Privilege and share in the combined good works of the entire Carmelite Order throughout the world and over 200 million members of the Scapular Confraternity.

Those who become associated with one of our neighborhood chapters will also receive the companionship and support of individuals holding like moral and spiritual convictions. In addition, our members will receive the great satisfaction of being able to make both their spiritual and temporal efforts count through their development of truly God-centered communities, which will nourish sound moral families in their local areas.

Those members who consecrate them-selves totally to the Holy Family (to Jesus, through Mary, in union with St. Joseph) will receive an abundance of grace by becoming the Holy Family's consecrated children.

Those who donate their time and resources to the Apostolate will receive many partial indulgences for their good works.

All members of the Apostolate are spiritually united with Mother Teresa of Calcutta and all Missionaries of Charity throughout the world. On April 22, 1978, Mother Teresa, who is a member of our Advisory Council, signed up all of the members of her community as Sacri-State members of the Apostolate for Family Consecration. Therefore, all members of the Apostolate are spiritually united with Mother Teresa's community, and many other communities and generous individuals throughout the world, who are praying and suffering for our work. Indeed, when you combine this powerhouse of prayer and sacrifice with the prayers of the many souls being released from Purgatory because of our practices, our goal to be used as an instrument of the Holy Family to transform neighborhoods into God-centered communities will certainly be accomplished.

Litany of the Sacred Heart of Jesus

L. Lord, have mercy on us.
A. Christ, have mercy on us.

L. Lord, have mercy on us.
Christ, hear us.
A. Christ, graciously hear us.

God, the Father of Heaven, *Have mercy on us.*

God the Son, Redeemer of the world, *Have mercy on us.*

God the Holy Ghost, *Have mercy on us.*

Holy Trinity, one God, *Have mercy on us.*

Heart of Jesus, Son of the Eternal Father, *Have mercy on us.*

Heart of Jesus, formed by the Holy Ghost in the Virgin Mother's womb, *Have mercy on us.*

Heart of Jesus, substantially united to the Word of God, *Have mercy on us.*

Heart of Jesus, of infinite majesty, *Have mercy on us.*

Heart of Jesus, holy temple of God, *Have mercy on us.*

Heart of Jesus, tabernacle of the Most High, *Have mercy on us.*

Heart of Jesus, house of God and gate of Heaven, *Have mercy on us.*

Heart of Jesus, glowing furnace
of charity, *Have mercy on us.*

Heart of Jesus, vessel of justice
and love, *Have mercy on us.*

Heart of Jesus, full of goodness
and love, *Have mercy on us.*

Heart of Jesus, abyss of all
virtues, *Have mercy on us.*

Heart of Jesus, most worthy of
all praise, and knowledge, *Have mercy on us.*

Heart of Jesus, wherein dwells
all the fullness of the Godhead, *Have mercy on us.*

Heart of Jesus, in Whom the
Father is wed, *Have mercy on us.*

Heart of Jesus, of Whose
fullness we have all received, *Have mercy on us.*

Heart of Jesus, desire of the
everlasting hills, *Have mercy on us.*

Heart of Jesus, patient and rich
in mercy, *Have mercy on us.*

Heart of Jesus, rich unto all who
call upon Thee, *Have mercy on us.*

Heart of Jesus, fount of life and
holiness, *Have mercy on us.*

Heart of Jesus, propitiation for
our offenses, *Have mercy on us.*

Heart of Jesus, overwhelmed
with reproaches, *Have mercy on us.*

Heart of Jesus, bruised for our
iniquities, *Have mercy on us.*

Heart of Jesus, obedient even unto death,	*Have mercy on us.*
Heart of Jesus, pierced with a lance,	*Have mercy on us.*
Heart of Jesus, source of all consolation,	*Have mercy on us.*
Heart of Jesus, our life and resurrection,	*Have mercy on us.*
Heart of Jesus, our peace and reconciliation,	*Have mercy on us.*
Heart of Jesus, victim for our sins,	*Have mercy on us.*
Heart of Jesus, salvation of those who hope in Thee,	*Have mercy on us.*
Heart of Jesus, hope of those who die in Thee,	*Have mercy on us.*
Heart of Jesus, delight of all Saints,	*Have mercy on us.*
Lamb of God, Who takest away the sins of the world,	*Spare us, O Lord.*
Lamb of God, Who takest away the sins of the world,	*Graciously hear us, O Lord.*
Lamb of God, Who takest away the sins of the world,	*Have mercy on us.*
Jesus, meek and humble of Heart,	*Make our hearts like unto Thine.*

Let us pray.

Almighty and everlasting God, look upon the Heart of Thy well-beloved Son and upon the praise and satisfaction which He offers unto Thee in the name of sinners; and do Thou of Thy great goodness grant them pardon when they seek Thy mercy, in the name of Thy Son, Jesus Christ, who liveth and reigneth with Thee for ever and ever. Amen.

The Litany of Our Lady of Loreto

L. Lord, have mercy on us.
A. Christ, have mercy on us.

L. Lord, have mercy on us.
Christ, hear us.
A. Christ, graciously hear us.

God the Father of Heaven,	*Have mercy on us.*
God the Son, Redeemer of the world,	*Have mercy on us.*
God the Holy Ghost,	*Have mercy on us.*
Holy Trinity, one God,	*Have mercy on us.*
Holy Mary,	*Pray for us.*
Holy Mother of God,	*Pray for us.*
Holy Virgin of virgins,	*Pray for us.*
Mother of Christ	*Pray for us.*
Mother of divine grace,	*Pray for us.*
Mother most pure,	*Pray for us.*
Mother most chaste,	*Pray for us.*
Mother inviolate,	*Pray for us.*
Mother undefiled,	*Pray for us.*

Mother most amiable,	*Pray for us.*
Mother most admirable,	*Pray for us.*
Mother of good counsel,	*Pray for us.*
Mother of our Creator,	*Pray for us.*
Mother of our Savior,	*Pray for us.*
Virgin most prudent,	*Pray for us.*
Virgin most venerable,	*Pray for us.*
Virgin most renowned,	*Pray for us.*
Virgin most powerful,	*Pray for us.*
Virgin most merciful,	*Pray for us.*
Virgin most faithful,	*Pray for us.*
Mirror of justice,	*Pray for us.*
Seat of wisdom,	*Pray for us.*
Cause of joy,	*Pray for us.*
Spiritual vessel,	*Pray for us.*
Vessel of honor,	*Pray for us.*
Singular vessel of devotion,	*Pray for us.*
Mystical rose,	*Pray for us.*
Tower of David,	*Pray for us.*
Tower of ivory,	*Pray for us.*
House of gold,	*Pray for us.*
Ark of the covenant,	*Pray for us.*

Gate of Heaven,	*Pray for us.*
Morning star,	*Pray for us.*
Health of the sick,	*Pray for us.*
Refuge of sinners,	*Pray for us.*
Comforter of the afflicted,	*Pray for us.*
Help of Christians,	*Pray for us.*
Queen of Angels,	*Pray for us.*
Queen of Patriarchs,	*Pray for us.*
Queen of Prophets,	*Pray for us.*
Queen of Apostles,	*Pray for us.*
Queen of Martyrs,	*Pray for us.*
Queen of Confessors,	*Pray for us.*
Queen of Virgins,	*Pray for us.*
Queen of all Saints,	*Pray for us.*
Queen conceived without original sin,	*Pray for us.*
Queen of the most holy Rosary,	*Pray for us.*
Queen of peace,	*Pray for us.*
Lamb of God, Who takest away the sins of the world,	*Spare us, O Lord.*
Lamb of God, Who takest away the sins of the world,	*Spare us, O Lord.*
Lamb of God, Who takest away the sins of the world,	*Graciously hear us, O Lord.*

Pray for us, O holy Mother of
God,

*That we may be
made worthy of the
promises of Christ.*

Let us pray.

Grant, we beseech Thee, O Lord God, unto us Thy
servants, that we may rejoice in continual health of mind
and body; and, by the glorious intercession of blessed
Mary ever Virgin, may be delivered from present
sadness, and enter into the joy of Thine eternal gladness.
Through Christ our Lord. Amen.

Litany of St. Joseph

Leader - Lord, have mercy on us.
All - Christ, have mercy on us.

Lord, have mercy on us;
Christ hear us,

*Christ, graciously
hear us.*

God, the Father of heaven,

*Have mercy on **us**.*

God, the Son, Redeemer of the
world,

Have mercy on us.

God, the Holy Spirit,

Have mercy on us.

Holy Trinity, One God,

Have mercy on us.

Holy Mary,

Pray for us.

St. Joseph,

*Pray for us (or)
thank you.*

Renowned offspring of David,

*Pray for us (or)
thank you.*

Splendor of Patriarchs,

*Pray for us (or)
thank you.*

Spouse of the Mother of God,	*Pray for us (or) thank you.*
Chaste guardian of the Virgin,	*Pray for us (or) thank you.*
Foster father of the Son of God,	*Pray for us (or) thank you.*
Watchful defender of Christ,	*Pray for us (or) thank you.*
Head of the Holy Family,	*Pray for us (or) thank you.*
Joseph most just,	*Pray for us (or) thank you.*
Joseph most pure,	*Pray for us (or) thank you.*
Joseph most prudent,	*Pray for us (or) thank you.*
Joseph most courageous,	*Pray for us (or) thank you.*
Joseph most obedient,	*Pray for us (or) thank you.*
Joseph most faithful,	*Pray for us (or) thank you.*
Mirror of patience,	*Pray for us (or) thank you.*
Lover of poverty,	*Pray for us (or) thank you.*
Model for all who work,	*Pray for us (or) thank you.*
Glory of family life,	*Pray for us (or) thank you.*

Guardian of virgins,	*Pray for us (or) thank you.*
Mainstay of families,	*Pray for us (or) thank you.*
Comfort of the afflicted,	*Pray for us (or) thank you.*
Hope of the sick,	*Pray for us (or) thank you.*
Patron of the dying,	*Pray for us (or) thank you.*
Terror of the demons,	*Pray for us (or) thank you.*
Protector of the Holy Church,	*Pray for us (or) thank you.*

Lamb of God, Who takest away
the sins of the world, *Spare us, O Lord.*

Lamb of God, Who takest away
the sins of the world, *Graciously hear us, O Lord.*

Lamb of God, Who takest away
the sins of the world. *Have mercy on us.*

He made him lord over His
household. *And ruler of all His possessions.*

Let us pray

My God, Who in Your unspeakable providence did
grant to choose blessed Joseph to be the spouse of Your
own most holy Mother, grant we beg You, that we may
have him for our mediator in heaven, whom we venerate
as our defender on earth, who lives and reigns world
without end. Amen.

Chaplet of the Divine Mercy

In the early 1930's, Sister M. Faustina, of the Congregation of the Sisters of Our Lady of Mercy, was visited by Our Lord and entrusted with a wonderful message of Mercy for all mankind.

> "Tell distressed mankind to nestle close to My merciful Heart, and I will fill them with peace ... Mankind will not find peace until it turns with confidence to My Mercy."

Jesus taught her to say this prayer on ordinary rosary beads:

First say one **'Our Father', 'Hail Mary'** *and* **'I believe'.**

Then on the large beads say the following words:

'Eternal Father, I offer You the Body and Blood, Soul and Divinity of Your dearly beloved Son, Our Lord Jesus Christ, in atonement for our sins and those of the whole world.'

On the smaller beads you are to say the following words:

'For the sake of His sorrowful Passion have mercy on us and on the whole world.'

After the five decades you are to say these words three times:

'Holy God, Holy Mighty One, Holy Immortal One, have mercy on us and on the whole world.' "

Jesus said later to Sister Faustina: "I want the whole world to know My infinite Mercy. I want to give unimaginable graces to those who trust in My Mercy."

Primarily responsible for the resurgence of the devotion to the Divine Mercy was the Archbishop of Sister Faustina's home diocese of Cracow, Poland, Karol Cardinal Wojtyla, now Pope John Paul II.

Jesus, I Trust in You!

Reply Section

1. ( ) Please place this petition at the foot of the altar in your Sacred Hearts Chapel and include it in all of the Masses said for the needs of your petitioners throughout the coming week. Also include these petitions in your vigil of prayer on Fridays, particularly on First Fridays when your president spends his day or night before Our Eucharistic Lord praying for the intentions of all petitions received throughout the month.

_____

_____

_____

_____

_____

_____

_____

_____

_____

_____

2.a ( ) I promise to pray that God will use The Apostolate to inspire people to become an instrument to renew the family and the entire world in Jesus Christ. I would like to be listed as a Sacri-State member and participate in the spiritual benefits of The Apostolate.

2b ( ) I am a priest, and will include the intentions of The Apostolate and all of those who are asking for your prayers in my available Masses, particularly on Fridays.

3. ( ) Enclosed is my best for God, my seed-Charity donation for the vital work of The Apostolate. _____

4. ( ) Enclosed is a list of names of people who should be interested in The Apostolate.

5. ( ) I am not on your mailing list, please add my name.

6. ( ) Please notify me when you start to organize chapters in my area.

7. ( ) I would like to receive more information about Cooperator membership.

8. ( ) Please send your order form for your prayer books and materials.

Please Print:

Name: _____

Address: _____

City & State: _____

Zip: _____

The Apostolate, Box 220, Kenosha, WI 53141

Reply Section

1. ( ) Please place this petition at the foot of the altar in your Sacred Hearts Chapel and include it in all of the Masses said for the needs of your petitioners throughout the coming week. Also include these petitions in your vigil of prayer on Fridays, particularly on First Fridays when your president spends his day or night before Our Eucharistic Lord praying for the intentions of all petitions received throughout the month.

_____

_____

_____

_____

_____

_____

_____

_____

_____

_____

2.a ( ) I promise to pray that God will use The Apostolate to inspire people to become an instrument to renew the family and the entire world in Jesus Christ. I would like to be listed as a Sacri-State member and participate in the spiritual benefits of The Apostolate.

2b ( ) I am a priest, and will include the intentions of The Apostolate and all of those who are asking for your prayers in my available Masses, particularly on Fridays.

3. ( ) Enclosed is my best for God, my seed-Charity donation for the vital work of The Apostolate. _____

4. ( ) Enclosed is a list of names of people who should be interested in The Apostolate.

5. ( ) I am not on your mailing list, please add my name.

6. ( ) Please notify me when you start to organize chapters in my area.

7. ( ) I would like to receive more information about Cooperator membership.

8. ( ) Please send your order form for your prayer books and materials.

Please Print:

Name: _____

Address: _____

City & State: _____

Zip: _____

The Apostolate, Box 220, Kenosha, WI 53141